# THE
# PATENT
# GUIDE

## A Friendly Guide to Protecting and Profiting from Patents

## by Carl W. Battle, Esq.
### Registered U.S. Patent Attorney

with contributing authors
**Jean B. Barish, Esq.**
**Craig M. Bell, Esq.**
**Michael P. Morris, Esq.**
**Vincent J. Napoleon, Esq.**
**Jonathan B. Penn, Esq.**

ALLWORTH PRESS
NEW YORK

Published by Allworth Press
An imprint of Allworth Communications
10 East 23rd Street, New York, NY 10010

Cover design by Douglas Designs, New York, NY

Book design by Sharp Des!gns, Holt, MI

ISBN: 1-880559-72-2

Library of Congress Catalog Card Number: 96-79670

Printed in Canada

# Contents

# Preface

CREATIVE PEOPLE ARE EVERYWHERE. From Microsoft's founder, Bill Gates, to the conventional garage or basement inventor, people like you are coming up with great ideas for products every day. These innovative ideas are essential to business and economic progress.

Have you had an idea for an invention or an innovative way of doing something that could improve productivity, create jobs, solve some long-standing problem, and make a lot of money for you and your supporters? Small inventors like you are the cornerstone of America's creativity and competitiveness.

Although coming up with a great idea or invention is often the biggest step, it is still only the first step. Several things remain to be done before you can expect to realize financial gain from your idea or invention. Many great ideas fail because the inventors do not take appropriate steps to protect, promote, and profit from their ideas.

You need to find out if your idea is original, or if someone has already produced it; there are many places you can check. Check stores and catalogs if your idea is for a consumer product. Check trade associations and trade publications in the field related to your idea or invention and visit relevant trade shows. If your idea or invention can be patented, make a patent search and consider filing a patent application to protect the invention.

The chances that you are the first or only person to think of a particular idea or invention may be small. Even if you are the first to produce "the better mousetrap," nobody is going to beat a path to your door for the product. You must devote the required time, effort, and money to make your idea or invention successful.

*The Patent Guide* provides basic and comprehensive information on patenting and marketing your ideas and inventions. This book includes an overview of methods for commercializing your invention, sources of information and assistance, easy-to-follow instructions, and advice on how to obtain a U.S. patent on your idea or invention. Topics such as information and guidance on using patent attorneys and agents, dealing with invention brokers and promotion firms, maintaining confidentiality of your ideas, obtaining foreign patent rights, enforcing your patent against infringement, licensing opportunities, and much more are also included.

The easy-to-use forms and step-by-step instructions allow you to handle patenting and commercializing your invention without hiring a patent attorney or invention broker. Depending on the complexity of the invention and your own skills, you may need the advice of a patent attorney or agent or marketing specialists. *The Patent Guide* provides information that can assist in the selection of an attorney or agent and can help you to get involved and monitor the patent and marketing process. Many expense-saving techniques are provided to help you minimize costs and maximize profits from your ideas and inventions.

# Introduction

NEW CONCEPTS AND IDEAS come in many forms: a new book, product name, machine, chemical composition, manufacturing process, medical treatment, and ornamental design. All of these are considered "intellectual property" or "property of the mind" and they can be bought, sold, licensed, and otherwise exploited like other personal property and real estate. How you can protect and profit from your idea depends on the type of idea it is, the kind of legal protection that is available, how concrete and developed your idea is, and how effectively you promote and market your idea.

A bare idea is usually not protected by patents, copyrights, trademarks, or any other form of intellectual property. A concept is difficult to protect, license, or market, unless it is in a tangible form. An invention must be reduced to practice before it can be patented. An idea must be created via some medium, such as a book, a videotape, or a sound recording, before it can be protected by copyright. Trademark rights ultimately require use of the mark with some good or service. Thus, an idea merely carried in your head is useful to no one.

Some people occasionally confuse patents, copyrights, and trademarks. Although the rights of patents, copyrights, and trademarks resemble each other, they are different and serve different purposes.

A U.S. patent for an invention is a grant of a property right by the government, acting through the U.S. Patent and Trademark Office (PTO), to the inventor, or his or her heirs or assigns. The right conferred by the patent grant extends throughout the United States and its territories and possessions. The right conferred by the patent grant is the right to exclude others from making, using, selling, offering for sale, or importing the invention. A patent does not grant the owner the right to make, use, or sell the invention, but the right to exclude others from making, using, or selling the invention. The term of the patent is seventeen years from the date the patent is granted on applications filed before June 8, 1995, or twenty years from the date of first filing on applications filed on or after June 8, 1995. The term of the patent is subject to the payment of periodic maintenance fees.

Since the essence of the right granted by a U.S. patent is the right to exclude others from commercial use of the invention, the patent owner is the only one who may make, use, or sell his or her invention. Others cannot do so without authorization from the patent owner. Thus, a patent owner can choose to manufacture and sell the invention or can license others to do so. Detailed information on patents is presented later in this book.

A copyright protects writings and other artistic creations of an author against copying. Literary, dramatic, musical, and artistic works are included within the protection of the copyright law, which in some instances also confers performing and recording rights. The copyright protects the form of expression rather than the subject matter of the writing. A description of a machine could be copyrighted as a writing, but this would only prevent others from copying the description. The copyright would not prevent others from writing a description of their own or from making and using the machine. Copyrights are registered in the U.S. Copyright Office in the Library of Congress. Chapter 2 provides a helpful overview of copyrights. Additional information concerning copyrights can be obtained from the Register of Copyrights, Library of Congress, Washington, D.C.

20559. (Telephone 202/707-3000). Detailed information on copyrights can be found in *The Copyright Guide* (Allworth Press, 1996).

A trademark relates to any word, name, symbol, or device that is used in trade with goods. The trademark indicates the source or origin of the goods and distinguishes the goods from the goods of others. Trademark rights can prevent others from using a confusingly similar mark but do not prevent others from making the same goods or from selling the goods under a nonconfusing mark. Similar rights can be acquired in service marks, which are used in the sale or advertising of services. Trademarks and service marks, which are used in interstate or foreign commerce, can be registered in the PTO. Basic information on trademarks is provided in chapter 2. Additional information on trademarks is available in *The Trademark Guide* (Allworth Press, 1996).

Before introducing the basics of patenting your invention, *The Patent Guide* provides a requisite overview of how to make your ideas and inventions a success. The first thought of many inventors is to present their ideas to a big national company. If you do approach a company or anyone else about your idea, ask them to sign a confidentiality agreement. The confidentiality agreement obligates the other party to maintain your idea in confidence and to not use or disclose it without your permission. If the other party refuses to sign a nondisclosure agreement, file a patent application for your invention before disclosing it. Present written terms to the other party, nevertheless, that any disclosures you make are in confidence and you expect compensation if your invention is used. Important information on how to maintain the confidentiality of your idea or invention is provided in chapter 6.

You may be able to produce your idea or invention yourself. Working from your home and selling items by mail order is a good way to get started. If you can start (or already have started) your own company, you will usually be better off because selling your company may be easier than promoting an idea or patent to a larger company; even if your company is losing money. Starting a business to market your invention is discussed in chapter 13.

Between the extremes of starting your own company and selling your company to a big business is taking your idea to small and medium-sized businesses. Such firms may be happy to produce an item that sells in amounts too small to interest large companies. Thus, a small firm may be more able and interested in trying to make your idea a reality.

Once you have looked at issues such as originality, production, distribution, and marketability, it's time to consider protecting your idea. If you do have a patentable idea, look into protecting it under the patent laws.

To document your invention, ask a close friend who understands your invention to sign his or her name on a dated diagram or written description of it, or file a disclosure document or a provisional patent application with the PTO. Taking one of these measures will provide evidence of the time you came up with your invention in case of a dispute with other inventors over who conceived the idea first. Filing a disclosure document with the PTO does not give you patent protection, but it does provide evidence of your invention. Sending yourself a registered letter describing the invention is useless as evidence.

Make a patent search to find out if the invention has already been patented. Chapter 7 provides information on determining the patentability of your invention. Search on a computerized database of patents, such as LEXIS, or at the PTO in Crystal Plaza, Arlington, Virginia. The staff at the PTO will assist in conducting patent searches and in using the facilities of the office. If your invention is complex or involves complicated issues, you may need the help of a patent agent or patent attorney to review the search results to determine whether your invention is patentable. Chapter 5 explains the details of using patent agents and attorneys.

If the invention has not already been patented or publicly known for more than one year, you can prepare a patent application and file it with the PTO. Specific information on preparing and filing a simple U.S. patent application is presented in chapter 8.

A U.S. utility patent can be obtained on a new, useful, and unobvious process; machine; article of manufacture; or composition of matter; or a new and useful improvement of any of these.

A valid patent cannot be obtained if (1) the invention has been described in a printed publication anywhere in the world or if it has been in public use or on sale in the United States before the date that you made your invention, or (2) the invention has been described in a printed publication anywhere, or has been in public use, or has been on sale in the United States for more than one year. In this connection, it is immaterial when the invention was made, or whether the printed publication or public use was by you or by someone else. If you described the invention in a printed publication or used the invention publicly or placed it on sale, you must apply for a patent within one year, otherwise any right to a patent will be lost.

If you can show that your invention performs a function, it will easily meet the usefulness test. An invention can be useful even if it is destructive. For example, a gun, or explosive, is patentable though its primary purpose is to kill or destroy.

Typically, the most difficult requirement in establishing patentability is whether the invention is obvious. A patent cannot be obtained even though the invention is not identically disclosed or described in the prior art, if the differences between the invention and the prior art are such that the subject matter as a whole would have been obvious, at the time the invention was made, to a person having ordinary skill in the art to which the subject matter pertains.

Even if the subject matter sought to be patented is not exactly shown by the prior art and involves one or more differences over the most similar thing already known, a patent may still be refused if the differences would be obvious. The subject matter sought to be patented must be sufficiently different from what has been used or described before so that it may be said to amount to invention over the prior art. Small advances that would be obvious to a person having ordinary skill in the art are not considered inventions capable of being patented. For example, the substitution of one material for another, or changes in size, are ordinarily not patentable.

If an inventor is merely utilizing the teachings or suggestions of the published literature or prior art to solve a problem and no unexpected results are obtained, it is doubtful that the invention will overcome the obviousness test. The invention must be evaluated on the basis of how it relates to a problem, how it creates a solution, how it differs from prior art, and how commercially successful it might be.

Policy can prevent certain inventions from being patentable.

Methods of doing business and printed matter cannot be patented. Inventions useful solely in the use of special nuclear material or atomic energy for atomic weapons are excluded from patent protection by the Atomic Energy Act. Remember that a patent cannot be obtained on a mere idea or suggestion; rather, a complete description and reduction to practice of the invention is required.

In addition to the utility patent discussed above, a design or plant patent can be obtained. A design patent can be granted to a person who has invented any new, original, and ornamental design for an article of manufacture. The design patent is effective for fourteen years and protects the appearance of an article but not features of structure or utility. A plant patent can be granted to anyone who has invented or discovered and asexually reproduced any distinct and new variety of plant. This includes cultivated sports, mutants, hybrids, and newly found seedlings, other than a plant found in an uncultivated state or a tuber-propagated plant such as the Irish potato.

Specific review and helpful advice on all issues regarding the patenting process are presented later. This includes information such as how to obtain foreign patent rights, how to enforce your patent against infringers, and what are the licensing opportunities for your patents and inventions.

While you probably still have to invest considerable time, money, and effort in your invention, you can get help from a number of sources. Patent attorneys and agents can help you make a patent search and file and prosecute a patent application, if you cannot do this yourself. Invention promoters are firms that offer—for a fee— to take on the whole job of protecting and promoting you idea. Invention brokers work for a portion of the profits from an invention. Invention brokers may help inventors raise capital and form companies to produce and market their inventions, and they often provide sophisticated management advice.

Other sources of help include invention and entrepreneurial centers located at university campuses. The National Science Foundation funds some centers and provides assistance for inventors and innovators. The Small Business Administration's (SBA) Small Business Institutes (SBI) are located at several hundred colleges and universities around the country, and they may provide the market research, feasibility analysis, and business planning necessary to make an invention successful. The Office of Energy-Related Inventions in the U.S. Department of Commerce's National Bureau of Standards sometimes evaluates—free of charge—non-nuclear energy-related inventions and ideas for devices, materials, and procedures.

Inventor's clubs, associations, and societies are useful sources for networking, gathering information about patenting and promoting your ideas and inventions. Such organizations might be located in your area. Talking with other inventors is probably the most helpful thing you can do. Don't forget that a big part of being successful with your ideas and invention will involve being informed, learning from experience, and networking with others for advice and assistance.

# CHAPTER 1

# Making Your Ideas and Inventions a Success

THERE ARE SEVERAL WAYS that you can profit from your idea or invention. Realize that there is no magic formula for success with any idea and no certainty that any approach will guarantee your expectations of success. What's important is that you review and analyze all available options and take steps toward your goal. Your main objective is to realize a financial gain from your idea or invention, not to merely patent, copyright, or trademark it. Keep in mind, however, that protecting your idea or invention can be extremely important to your ability to profit from it.

Evaluating the marketability and commercial potential of your idea or invention is important. Although this commercial evaluation is a continuous and ongoing process, the process should start before you invest time and money in an idea that may not have salability. All too often people spend countless hours and thousands of dollars on ideas that are not commercially feasible. The world may not want your "better mousetrap" if it is too expensive to build or maintain, or if there are no more mice to catch.

Don't fall into the trap of thinking that because you are the first to think of an idea, or the first to patent it, that you will be guaranteed fame and fortune. Nothing could be further from the truth. Less than 5 percent of all patented inventions make money, and the percentage is even lower for small, independent inventors. Big corporations can spend millions of dollars on research and development before finding a commercial success, whereas the small inventor typically cannot afford to do so.

There are several approaches for evaluating the commercial potential of your invention. You can start by checking trade publications and trade shows in fields that relate to your invention. Learn what other inventors have tried and whether their attempts failed or succeeded. Visit the library and search catalogs and product directories for information about inventions similar to yours. Contact inventor's clubs and organizations and talk to other inventors about problems and solutions in the field of your invention. Attend workshops and classes at universities and community colleges covering the subject matter of your invention, and talk to instructors about consumer and business needs for inventions such as yours. Consult with buyers and sales personnel in stores and shops which carry articles and devices that are similar or related to your invention. Talk to technical people, scientists and engineers, who work in relevant fields to determine if there is a real need for your invention.

Be careful about discussing or disclosing your invention to others without taking proper precautions to protect its confidentiality and proprietary nature. Before discussing or showing your invention to others, ask them to sign a confidentiality agreement wherein they agree to keep your invention a secret and not use the invention without your permission. This confidentiality agreement is extremely important in order to protect your ability to obtain foreign patents on your invention, because any public disclosure, sale, or use of your invention before filing a patent application will preclude you from patenting the invention in most foreign countries that require absolute novelty. Unlike most foreign countries, the United States provides a one-year grace period to file a patent application after public disclosure or sale of the invention.

Never disclose your unpatented invention to any person or

company that you do not trust. Rather, always try to deal with ethical and reputable organizations in discussing, evaluating, and testing your invention. Even reputable organizations may refuse to sign a confidentiality agreement before reviewing your invention. Despite this, it may be necessary for you to disclose your invention to these firms to exploit the invention commercially. If you are unable to get the other party to sign a confidentiality agreement, you should still indicate in your initial contact and in a follow-up letter that your invention was disclosed in confidence, and you expect that it will not be used without your permission and compensation. Refer to chapter 6 for further details on maintaining the confidentiality of your invention.

Documentation of your idea or invention is important in protecting your rights. Write a description and create a drawing (if applicable) of your idea or invention as soon as you have conceived your idea. Sign and date this documentation and also and have it read, signed, and dated by one or more witnesses who did not contribute to the conception of the invention. This documentation can be crucial to prove inventorship and the date thereof, in case of a dispute over who invented the item first.

You can also file an Invention Disclosure Document with the U.S. Patent and Trademark Office (PTO) to document your invention for a small fee. The PTO will keep the Disclosure Document on file for two years, or longer if you file a patent application making reference to it, and you can rely on this Disclosure Document to prove the date of conception of your invention. Be aware, however, that the Disclosure Document does not protect your invention from being copied by others.

Another way to document your invention and gain some time to evaluate and test it is to file a provisional patent application with the PTO. A provisional patent application is an abbreviated version of a regular patent application and is useful in establishing an early filing date for a subsequent regular patent application. Filing a provisional patent application is about one-fifth of the cost of a regular application and can save you money up front. Additionally, filing a provisional patent application allows you time to review the commercial potential of your invention. A provisional patent application will not issue as a patent unless within one year you either convert it to a regular patent application or file a separate regular patent application claiming the benefit of the provisional application.

Thorough documentation of your invention can also be helpful in proving theft of your invention and in avoiding disputes over ownership of the invention. For example, if someone steals your invention, convincing documentary evidence will be the key in showing that you made the invention first and that the other party stole or derived it from you. An inventor often makes an invention while working for a company or is employed by a company after making an invention. In many cases, the company requires the employee to sign an employment agreement giving the company rights to any inventions made during the employment. Even without an employment agreement, a company typically has the right to freely use inventions made by employees on company time or with company resources. Again, proper documentation will be crucial in such cases in proving that the employee made the invention before starting his or her employment or without using company time or resources.

There are several major issues that must be addressed before you can be successful with your idea or invention. Is your idea or invention original, or has someone already tried it? Can you or someone else produce and distribute your invention if it is a new product? If your idea or invention is a new process, or new application for an existing product, can it be put to effective use? Will someone buy your idea or invention, and will it really make money? Can you protect your idea or invention by a patent or in any other way?

In resolving the above issues, there are a number of related factors that must be considered. The Small Business Administration (SBA) has provided the following list of areas that might be evaluated for each new idea or invention:

| | |
|---|---|
| legality | usage learning |
| safety | product visibility |
| environmental impact | service |
| societal impact | durability |
| potential market | functional feasibility |
| product life cycle | production feasibility |

development status

investment costs

product line potential

need

promotion

appearance

price

protection

payback period

profitability

product interdependence

research and development

trend of demand

stability of demand

consumer/user compatibility

marketing research

distribution

perceived function

existing competition

new competition

potential sales

This list is not intended to discourage you with your invention but to highlight the myriad of variables that may have to be considered before your invention can be successfully commercialized.

As mentioned earlier, consider all available options in trying to profit from your invention. This is no time for linear thinking, because there is no guaranteed route to success. Look at the merits of manufacturing and marketing the invention yourself, selling or licensing the invention to a large company, or working with a small or medium-sized company to produce your product. Remember that starting your own small business to sell the product of your invention is usually better than trying to sell or license the unmarketed invention to another company. Selling a business is usually easier than selling an idea or a patent. Prospective buyers are likely to understand a business much better than they would the technical details of your invention. Many businesspeople are likely to believe that they have better business and marketing skills than you as an inventor and can make the product profitable, if you have a good product. Also, many of them typically feel that when they purchase a business, some customers already exist and that most of the bugs have been worked out of the product.

You can consider selling or licensing your invention to a major company. After all, a big company usually has the funds, manufacturing capability, and marketing expertise to commercialize the invention and make it profitable. Most major companies, however, are usually not interested in unsolicited ideas from people outside of the company. In fact, many companies do not accept or consider outside ideas. First, they believe that their own research and development staff can do a better job at inventing than an independent inventor working out of a basement or garage. Second, they are afraid that outside ideas or inventions will conflict with their own in-house research efforts. Many companies have become involved in expensive lawsuits with outside inventors to prove that the companies were already developing the disputed invention. Third, many ideas and inventions from outside inventors are simply too small in potential sales to interest large corporations. For example, your niche market of one million dollars in potential sales is typically not appealing to a big company that is looking for tens or hundreds of millions of dollars in sales. Thus, trying to interest a large company in your invention will be extremely difficult.

Invention brokers or invention promotion firms, with a proven track record, may be helpful in getting your idea considered by a big company. These firms may already have established relationships with large corporations, investment capitalists, or other organizations interested in new ideas. Be careful when using invention promotion firms because many of them are a sham. Federal Trade Commission (FTC) investigations found that several invention promotion firms, charging fees of several thousand dollars, had more than 30,000 clients and fewer than a dozen of these clients made money on their inventions. See chapter 4 for more information about invention brokers and invention promotion firms.

Besides starting your own business to market your invention or selling your business to a big company, you should consider taking your invention to a small or medium-sized company. These firms may be easier to approach than a big corporation, and they would be more likely to market a product with smaller sales volumes. Smaller companies may not be as sophisticated with marketing and distribution, but they can still successfully commercialize your invention and make it profitable.

Keep in mind that you need to be more than an idea person to be successful with your inventions. You need to be an entrepreneur, one who invents a product, finds backers for the product, and gets the product on the market. You need to be good at communication, negotiation, publicity, and networking. Most of all, you need to have persistence and good business sense.

# CHAPTER 2

# What Can Be Done to Protect Your Ideas

ONCE YOU HAVE come up with an idea, no matter how simple it is or what type it is, you should always look at ways to protect it. Your ideas and creations are valuable property that you can protect, defend, sell, license, mortgage, or otherwise transfer for economic benefit. Just as you can build a fence or install an alarm system to protect your home, you can protect intellectual property rights to your ideas by means of patents, trademarks, copyrights, and/or trade secrets.

The term "intellectual property" refers to any creation or product of the mind. This includes ideas, inventions, methods of doing business, industrial processes, artistic works, writings, product names, distinctive packaging, chemical formulas, and anything else that is created by mental processes. The type of intellectual property you have created will determine what type of protection you can obtain for it. The five basic forms of protection for intellectual property are patents, copyrights, trademarks, trade secrets, and protection from unfair trade practices. These forms of protection for intellectual property are not mutually exclusive and often overlap.

People typically confuse the types of intellectual property protection without realizing that each is distinct and protects specific subject matter. A preliminary introduction to patents, copyrights, and trademarks was provided earlier in this book. A detailed review of the forms of protection for intellectual property follows. This review will help you develop methodologies for assessing your ideas and inventions and for seeking the maximum protection for your intellectual property.

## Protecting Your Invention with Patents

Perhaps the best form of intellectual property protection for your invention is a patent. A patent gives the patent owner the legally enforceable right to exclude others from making, using, selling, and importing the patented invention. A patent owner enjoys a presumption of validity of his or her patent and monopoly with regard to the patented invention for the life of the patent.

Anyone who makes an invention can apply for a patent, no matter what age, national origin, mental capacity, or other traits. The inventor can file for a patent whether or not he or she is represented by a patent attorney or agent. Patents, once properly obtained, are usually given great deference by industry and the courts.

The patent is issued by the government through the PTO. An official printed copy of the patent with specification, drawing, and claims is provided to the patentee. The patent confers the right to exclude others from making, using, or selling the invention throughout the Unites States and its territories and possessions for the term of the patent subject to the payment of maintenance fees as provided by law.

The exact nature of the right conferred is the right to exclude. The patent does not grant the right to make, use, or sell the invention, but only grants the exclusive nature of the right. The patent only grants the right to exclude others from making, using, selling, offering for sale, or importing the invention. Since the patent does not grant the affirmative right to make, use, or sell the invention, the patentee's own right to do so is dependent upon the rights of others and any general laws that might be applicable.

A patentee, merely because he or she has received a patent for an invention, is not thereby authorized to make, use, or sell the invention if doing so would violate any law. An inventor of a new automobile who has obtained a patent thereon would not be entitled to use the patented automobile in violation of state laws requiring a license to operate the automobile, nor may a patentee sell an article the sale of which may be forbidden by a law, merely because a patent has been obtained. A patentee may not make, use, or sell his or her own invention if doing so would infringe the patent rights of others. A patentee, by virtue of having a patent, may not violate the pure food and drug laws or federal antitrust laws through resale price agreements or restraints of trade. Otherwise, there is nothing that prohibits a patentee from making, using, or selling his or her own invention.

Since the essence of the right granted by a patent is the right to exclude others from commercial exploitation of the invention, the patentee is the only one who can commercially exploit it. Others may not commercially exploit the invention without authorization from the patentee. The patentee may manufacture and sell the invention or may license or otherwise permit others to do so.

According to the law, only the inventor may apply for a patent, although there are some exceptions. If a person who is not the inventor applied for a patent, any patent obtained would be invalid. The person applying in such a case, who falsely states that he or she is the inventor, would be subject to criminal penalties. If the inventor is dead, the application for patent may be made by legal representatives, such as the administrator or executor of the estate. If the inventor is insane, the application for patent may be made by a guardian. If an inventor refuses to apply for a patent or cannot be found, a joint inventor or a person having a proprietary interest in the invention may apply on behalf of the missing inventor.

If two or more persons make an invention, they apply for a patent as joint inventors. A person who makes a financial contribution is not a joint inventor and cannot be listed in the application as an inventor. An innocent mistake in erroneously omitting an inventor or in erroneously naming a person as an inventor can be corrected on the application.

The patent law specifies the subject matter that can be patented and the conditions under which a patent may be obtained. The law provides that any person who invents or discovers any new and useful process, machine, article of manufacture, or composition of matter, or any new and useful improvements thereof, may obtain a patent, subject to the conditions and requirements of the law. A process is defined as a process, method, or set of steps. A machine is a device or equipment for performing physical functions. Articles of manufacture are goods and products that are made, and includes all manufactured articles. Compositions of matter are chemical compositions and may include mixtures of ingredients, as well as new chemical compounds. These classes of subject matter include practically everything made by man and the processes for making them.

A patent cannot be granted for mixtures of ingredients, such as medicines, unless there is more to the mixture than the known effect of its components. The mixture must have synergy or some unexpected advantage to be patentable. Remember, a patent cannot be obtained for a mere idea or suggestion. A complete description of the actual machine or other subject matter sought to be patented is required.

The three types of patents that you may be able to obtain on an invention are a utility patent, design patent, and a plant patent. The common type of patent is a utility patent, which covers the utilitarian features of an invention. Utility patents include patents on the functional characteristics of machines, apparatus, electronic devices, manufacturing processes, chemical compounds and compositions, medical treatments, manufactured articles, and the like. If other requirements for patentability are met, consider obtaining a utility patent on the functional and operational features of your invention.

The utility patent is perhaps the more difficult type of patent to obtain. To receive a utility patent on your invention, you have to file a patent application that includes a detailed description (including best mode of practicing the invention) of how to make and use the invention, claims that define the specific elements to be protected, drawings of the invention where necessary to help understand it, an abstract, a formal inventor's declaration, and the required filing fee. A utility patent protects the claimed invention from infringing items that literally tread on the patent claims, as well as others that are substantially similar under the "doctrine of equivalents." A sample utility patent is shown at the end of this chapter.

A design patent protects the shape or ornamental or artistic features of an article. Unlike a utility patent, a design patent does not protect the functional elements of an invention. If a design has functionality, then it cannot be protected by a design patent, even if the design is also ornamental. Some examples of designs that can be patented are unique bottle shapes, a computer screen display, an artistic lamp, an ornamental pin, a watch design, and the grill of an automobile.

A design patent has a fourteen-year term and protects against any design that is substantially similar to the patented design. A design patent is relatively easy to obtain if the design is new and nonfunctional. A design patent application is also simple to prepare and should include a preamble, a specification that explains the design, a single claim, one or more drawings, a formal inventor's declaration, and the filing fee. A sample design patent is presented at the end of this chapter.

You can file for a design patent and a utility patent on the same article. The design patent would be directed to the exterior appearance of the article whereas the utility patent would be directed to the function of the article. You can also copyright your unique design, in addition to obtaining a patent on it. Thus, one form of patent or intellectual property coverage does not preclude another. Be sure to consider all the available options for protecting your invention.

The law also provides for the granting of a patent to anyone who has invented or discovered and asexually reproduced any distinct and new variety of plant, including cultivated sports, mutants, hybrids, and newly found seedlings, other than a tuber-propagated plant or a plant found in an uncultivated state. Asexually propagated plants are those that reproduced by means other than from seeds such as by the rooting of cuttings, layering, budding, grafting, in arching, etc.

With reference to tuber-propagated plants, for which a plant patent cannot be obtained, the term "tuber" is used in its narrow, horticultural sense as meaning a short, thickened portion of an underground branch. The only plants covered by the term "tuber-propagated" are the Irish potato and the Jerusalem artichoke.

An application for a plant patent consists of the same parts as a utility patent application, as discussed earlier.

## Protecting Your Creations by Copyright

Obtaining a copyright is another way to protect your artistic, literary, software, or other creative works. Unlike a patent that covers the idea, a copyright covers only your particular form of expression of the idea.

A copyright gives you the sole right to control the reproduction and distribution of your copyrighted work. You have the right to prevent others from reproducing the work without your permission.

Copyright does not prevent others from using the ideas or information revealed by your work. Copyright protects only the literary, musical, artistic, or graphic form in which you express your work. Anyone is free to use your concepts and create his or her own expression of the same concepts as long as he or she does not copy your form of expression. Copyright protection does not extend to names, titles, and slogans. These can be appropriately protected by trademark.

Always review your creative works to see if they can be protected by copyright. The federal copyright law permits copyright protection for the following seven types of original works of authorship:
- literary works
- musical works, including any accompanying words
- dramatic works, including any accompanying music
- pantomimes and choreographic works
- pictorial, graphic, and sculptural works
- motion pictures and other audiovisual works
- sound recordings

Literary works are works, other than audiovisual works, that are expressed in words, numbers, or other verbal or numerical symbols such as books, magazines, manuscripts, directories, catalogs, cards, and computer programs. Musical works include written musical arrangements, lyrics, and songs.

Dramatic works include written plays and any written music that is a part thereof. Pantomimes and choreographic works include physical expressions and dance.

Pictorial, graphic, and sculptural works include two- and three-dimensional works of art, photographs, paintings, sketches, prints, maps, globes, charts, designs, technical drawings, diagrams, and models. Motion picture and audiovisual works include films, movies, and video recordings.

Sound recordings, such as discs, tapes, and phono records, are works that result from fixation of a series of musical, spoken, or other sounds but do not include the sounds accompanying a motion picture or other audiovisual work. Works not listed above may also be protected by copyright if they meet the definition of "original works of authorship."

Copyright protection is only available for original works of authorship. The originality requirement means that the work must be the independent creation of the person seeking copyright protection. The test for originality is met if the work owes its origin to the author and was independently created and not copied from other works. The mere fact that someone else has created something similar will not prevent you from obtaining copyright protection on your independent creation.

The works of authorship must be fixed in a tangible form to qualify for federal copyright protection. The work must be in a form that it can be reproduced or otherwise communicated. Thus, a mere idea or other abstract and imaginary creations cannot be protected by copyright.

A copyright originates automatically when the work is created, and registration is not required for copyright to exist. Your rights to enforce copyright, however, are maximized if the copyright is registered with the U.S. Copyright Office.

You can register your copyright by filing an application with the Copyright Office. This involves filing the appropriate application form along with the required fee and deposit of your work. Detailed instructions for completing the copyright application and a copy of Form TX, which is used for registering nondramatic literary works, are provided at the end of this chapter. The instructions are also useful for Forms PA, SR, and VA, which are applicable for works of performing arts, sound recording, and visual arts, respectively.

A copyright is good for fifty years after the life of the author. For a work-made-for-hire via employment or contract, the copyright is good for the lesser of seventy-five years after publication or one hundred years after creation.

Some areas where copyrights and patents overlap include the shapes and designs of containers, devices, and apparatus; toys and games; and computer software. Remember that an artistic bottle shape, for example, can be protected by a copyright and a design patent. A board game can be covered by a utility patent; the ornamental game board can be covered by a design patent and a copyright; and the rules, instructions, and packaging can be covered by copyright. Computer software can be protected by copyright, or it can be patented in conjunction with a process or some physical article, device, or apparatus. Now you see how copyrights and patents interface, and why you should consider them in protecting creative works.

For additional information on copyrights refer to *The Copyright Guide* (Allworth Press, 1996).

## Protecting Trademarks and Trade Dress

Trademarks are probably the most commonly known type of intellectual property because we encounter them every day. Popular trademarks, such as Xerox®, Coca Cola®, Listerine®, Plexiglas®, and GE® logo, are part of life in our home, in the office, or in public. Trademarks have become powerful forms of intellectual property protection with each mark worth hundreds of millions of dollars.

Trademarks may also be important in protecting certain aspects of your proprietary ideas and invention. Although trademarks will not protect the idea or invention itself, they can protect a proprietary name or symbol used with goods or services. Often the success of a product depends more on its name and packaging than on the product itself.

A trademark indicates the origin or source of goods or services; it symbolizes or guarantees the quality of the goods that bear the mark. A trademark is any work, name, symbol, device, or any combination thereof, adopted and used by a manufacturer or merchant to identify his or her goods and to distinguish them from those manufactured or sold by others. Rights in a trademark are acquired only by use of the trademark on particular goods. The right to use a trademark is a property interest that the trademark owner can assert to prevent others from using the mark, or from using one that is confusingly similar.

Federal registration of a trademark is not mandatory, but it does provide major benefits to the trademark owner. To be eligible for federal registration, a trademark must actually be used in commerce or the owner must have a bona fide intent to use the trademark in commerce. The intent to use the trademark can be extended for periods of six months up to a maximum of two years: intent is a good way of reserving a trademark with the PTO. A trademark is deemed to be used in commerce when it is placed in any manner on goods or on containers, tags, or labels affixed thereto, and the goods are sold or transported in interstate commerce.

Federal registration of a trademark protects the exclusive right of the trademark owner to use the mark nationwide. Federal registration also gives the trademark owner the right to use the registration symbol ®, which may deter others from using the mark. Additionally, the trademark owner has the right to sue unauthorized users of the trademark for an injunction, damages, or recovery of profits. If the trademark has not been registered, you should use the symbol ™ to protect your trademark rights under state law.

The U.S. trademark laws provide for the registration of trademarks on two types of registers: the Principal Register and the Supplemental Register. Trademarks that are created, arbitrary, or fanciful can, if otherwise qualified, be registered on the Principal Register. A trademark that does not qualify for registration on the Principal Register can be registered on the Supplemental Register provided the applicant shows that the mark is capable of distinguishing the applicant's goods and has been used in commerce for at least one year.

If all other requirements are satisfied, a trademark may be registered on the Principal Register unless it consists of a mark that (1) when applied to the applicant's goods or services is merely descriptive or deceptively misdescriptive of them; (2) when applied to the applicant's goods or services is primarily geographically descriptive or deceptively misdescriptive; or (3) is primarily a surname.

As an exception to the general rules, marks may be registered on the Principal Register if they have become distinctive as applied to the applicant's goods in commerce. This usually requires proof by the applicant of exclusive and continuous use of the mark in commerce for the prior five years.

The owner of a trademark that is used, or is intended to be used, in commerce may register the mark by filing an application for registration with the PTO. The application must be filed in the name of the trademark owner and comprise a written application, a drawing of the mark, three specimens or facsimiles of the mark, and the filing fee ($245 for registration in each class at the time of this printing). A sample trademark application is provided at the end of this chapter.

The PTO will allow registration of your trademark if all application requirements have been met and if your mark is not confusingly similar to other marks. If your application indicated a bona fide intent to use the mark, you must normally file a statement of actual use (along with dates of actual use, three specimens, and the required fee) within six months after receiving a notice of allowance from the PTO. The mark is published for opposition after allowance is granted, and, if no opposition is filed, the mark is registered.

Distinctive packaging or trade dress, in addition to unique advertising slogans, colors, jingles, architecture, or business designs, can also provide proprietary rights related to your product. Your use of these can give you offensive rights to stop others from using similar techniques that are likely to cause confusion with your products or services in the marketplace.

When creating a new product or service, always try to make the product name, packaging, and trade dress as unique and distinctive as possible. This uniqueness gives these features secondary meaning that is important in acquiring and enforcing trademark and unfair competition rights.

## Maintaining Trade Secret Rights

Keeping your idea or invention a trade secret may be another means of protecting valuable proprietary rights.

A trade secret is generally defined as:

> A trade secret may consist of any formula, pattern, device, or compilation of information which is or can be used in one's business, and which gives one an opportunity to obtain an advantage over competitors who do not know or use it, and which the law protects from misappropriation by others.

The subject matter covered by trade secret protection is broad. Almost any information or method used in business can be a trade secret if it is not generally known and if proper precautions are taken to maintain secrecy. For example, trade secrets can be applied to a formula, pattern, compilation, program, device, technique, process, customer lists, business plans, methods of doing business, and more.

The subject matter of a trade secret must be secret. Matters of public knowledge or of general knowledge in an industry cannot be appropriated by one as a trade secret. Matters that are disclosed by the goods that one markets cannot be a trade secret.

There are no precise rules for determining the existence of a trade secret. Rather, there are a number of factors that courts consider in deciding to recognize a trade secret. Usually, a trade secret must be novel and not generally known outside the holder of the trade secret. Courts generally do not require absolute secrecy, but a substantial element of secrecy must exist so that the information is not in the public domain.

Courts require the possessor of a trade secret to take reasonable measures to protect the secret. If reasonable and appropriate precautions are not taken to prevent disclosure or observation of a trade secret, then trade secret protection may be lost.

Trade secrets are recognized even when the information has been disclosed to contractors, suppliers, and others dealing with the holder of the trade secret, provided that the information is disclosed under a secrecy agreement or other confidential relationship.

Information that has no commercial value generally cannot be the subject of trade secret protection. Information has value if it gives the owner an opportunity to obtain an advantage over competitors who do not know or use it. A trade secret can have value even if it is not currently being used so long as it has a potential use.

The amount of effort or money expended by the holder of a trade secret in developing the secret is a factor in determining whether a trade secret exists. The larger the expenditures, the more likely a court is to uphold trade secret protection.

Courts typically require that trade secret information be marked confidential, or in some similar fashion, and be kept under lock. Additionally, trade secret processes and equipment should be isolated (where possible) in a restricted area. If the information is readily ascertainable from sources available to others, or if it can be analyzed or reverse engineered from products on the market, it is generally not considered a trade secret.

## United States Patent [19]

### Nick et al.

| | |
|---|---|
| [11] | **Patent Number:** **4,699,792** |
| [45] | **Date of Patent:** **Oct. 13, 1987** |

[54] **SELF-ADHESIVE PLASTER CONTAINING MEDICATION**

[75] Inventors: Erích Nick, Pinneberg; Günter Guse, Hamburg; Bodo Asmussen, Ammerbek, all of Fed. Rep. of Germany

[73] Assignee: Beiersdorf AG, Hamburg, Fed. Rep. of Germany

[21] Appl. No.: 745,169

[22] Filed: Jun. 17, 1985

[30] **Foreign Application Priority Data**

Jun. 23, 1984 [DE] Fed. Rep. of Germany ....... 3423328

[51] Int. Cl.$^4$ ...................... A61F 13/02; A61L 15/03; A61L 15/06

[52] U.S. Cl. ................................. 424/446; 424/449; 604/896; 604/897; 604/307; 128/156; 428/355

[58] Field of Search ...................... 424/16, 19, 20, 21, 424/26, 27, 28, 78, 83, 443, 446, 449; 604/897, 896, 304, 307; 128/156; 156/327, 332, 334; 428/354, 355, 356

[56] **References Cited**

**U.S. PATENT DOCUMENTS**

4,390,027 6/1983 Alani et al. ........................ 604/307

**FOREIGN PATENT DOCUMENTS**

2743979 4/1979 Fed. Rep. of Germany .
3202775 3/1983 Fed. Rep. of Germany ........ 424/28

*Primary Examiner*—John Kight
*Assistant Examiner*—Nathan M. Nutter
*Attorney, Agent, or Firm*—John C. Smith, Jr.

[57] **ABSTRACT**

A self-adhesive medicinal plaster comprises a plurality of adhesive elements spaced from each other on a surface of a carrier web and a plurality of active ingredient elements, containing a medication, spaced from each other and from the active ingredient elements on the surface of the carrier web whereby the medicinal active ingredient composition is isolated from the adhesive composition.

**21 Claims, 2 Drawing Figures**

**FIG. 1**

**FIG. 2**

4,699,792

**1**

### SELF-ADHESIVE PLASTER CONTAINING MEDICATION

#### FIELD OF THE INVENTION

This invention relates to a self-adhesive plaster with medicinal active ingredient elements and adhesive elements spaced from each other on a carrier for transdermal application.

#### BACKGROUND OF THE INVENTION

Plasters for transdermal application of medicinal active ingredients are known. Transdermal plasters are commercially available and are described in a large number of publications and patents.

In one type of transdermal plaster the medicinal active ingredients are arranged in a reservoir which is shielded from the skin with a control membrane which releases a controlled amount of active ingredient onto the skin through this membrane. A disadvantage of this arrangement is that the active ingredient, reservoir constituents and membrane must be carefully matched with one another, and consequently this system cannot be employed for all medicinal active ingredients. In addition, the production of such a plaster is expensive due to the complicated assembly of the parts.

In another type of transdermal plaster the medicinal active ingredient is incorporated into the adhesive composition of the plaster. In this case also, it is necessary for the active ingredient and adhesive composition to be carefully matched with one another. Although these systems are simpler and more economical to produce, they unavoidably result in interactions between the active ingredient and adhesive especially since as a general rule adhesives do not consist of defined individual constituents but are diverse mixtures.

German Offenlegungsschrift No. 3,202,775 describes an adhesive plaster for transdermal application of an active ingredient in which the active ingredient is printed onto the adhesive surface of the plaster in the form of separate spaced elements. Although such a plaster is economical to produce it has serious disadvantages and has not found acceptance in practice. In particular, the interactions between the active ingredient and adhesive composition impair uniform long-term release of the active ingredient through the skin because of migration, either of the active ingredient into the adhesive composition or the plasticizer or plasticizer-like substance into the active ingredient element, depending on external influences such as temperature and moisture. Such a plaster cannot fulfill the strict regulations of governmental registration as a drug especially in respect of the required storage stability under possibly adverse conditions during which migration phenomena may take place over a prolonged period.

An object of the present invention is, accordingly, to provide a medicated self-adhesive plaster for transdermal application which does not have, or has only to a substantially lesser degree, the above-mentioned disadvantages of the prior art. In particular, a plaster is provided which on the one hand can be produced economically and on the other hand is free from problems of migration of adhesives into the medicinal active ingredient and vice versa, and in addition, as far as possible, avoids any type of interaction between the two components.

**2**

### SUMMARY OF THE INVENTION

The invention, accordingly, relates to a self-adhesive plaster with separate active ingredient elements on a carrier for transdermal application which is characterized in that adhesive elements are arranged spatially separate from the active ingredient elements on the carrier, the adhesive elements consisting of adhesive systems which can be processed as a dispersion, plastisol or organisol, and both the adhesive elements and the active ingredient elements being approximately cap-shaped and adhering to the carrier by their base.

It is particularly advantageous for the apex of the medicinal active ingredient and adhesive elements to have about the same height in relation to the carrier. A uniformly good contact of both types of elements to the surface of the skin is thereby achieved.

The plaster, according to the invention, is thus free from interaction between the medicated active ingredient and adhesive. The resulting advantages are, in particular, that adhesives of the dispersion-type and the like, which are known per se, can be used as the adhesive and that, on the other hand, the medicated active ingredient can be processed with suitable pharmaceutical auxiliaries which are used for fixing to the carrier, according to the invention, and for optimum diffusion of the active ingredient into the skin. It is therefore no longer necessary to develop a formulation of the adhesive to suit the particular medicinal active ingredient or, conversely, a formulation of the active ingredient to suit the adhesive. Rather, an exceptionally variable system results with which medicinal active ingredients of the most diverse types may be used for transdermal application.

Advantageously, both the adhesive elements and the medicinal active ingredient elements are each applied from dispersions with a high solids content by a printing process. Suitable printing processes are gravure printing processes and, in particular, screen printing processes which are distinguished by single handling and exceptional economy with precise arrangement of the elements on the carrier web.

The adhesive elements and the medicinal active ingredient elements are preferably arranged in a regular pattern due to the geometry of the screen printing devices. The caps preferably have a base diameter of up to about 5000 $\mu$m, in particular 200–500 $\mu$m. If desired, however, it is possible to produce larger caps.

Because of the spatial separation of the active ingredient and adhesive the adhesive can be any adhesive which is known per se and which does not irritate the skin and which can be processed as described above. Suitable adhesives are, inter alia, rubber, polyacrylic acid esters and polyisobutylene, if appropriate, together with tackifying resins. These adhesives are advantageously processed from aqueous, concentrated, thixotropic dispersions of adhesives, the solids content preferably being 55–65% by weight. Suitable examples are adhesives based on methyl acrylic acid esters with alkyl radicals of 4–18 carbon atoms, such as butyl acrylate, ethylhexyl acrylate or stearyl acrylate, cross-linked or noncross-linked, it being possible to effect cross-linking, if appropriate, by electron beam radiation.

The rotary screen printing process uses a rotating weldless, drum-shaped and perforated rotary screen. In the inner jacket, a mechanically or magnetically held round-edged or square doctor blade forces the dispersion into the drum through the perforations of the

4,699,792

**3**

screen wall onto the carrier web. The carrier web passes the drum at a speed corresponding to the peripheral speed of the rotating screen drum driven by a back-pressure roller against the outer cover of the screen drum. To produce the plasters according to the invention, two synchronously running screen printing units connected in series, which place the adhesive elements and then the active ingredient elements exactly alongside one another in accordance with the whole geometry of the screens, are used in a suitable manner. The size and dosage of the microsize areas of adhesive and active ingredient which form as caps can be accurately determined by the diameter of the screen perforations and the wall thicknss of the screen. The number of possibilities of the arrangement is unlimited, and the arrangement can be selected as desired. There is thus the additional economic advantage that the adhesive formulation and active ingredient formulation can be applied to the carrier web in a production line with a high dosage accuracy.

The dispersions should be gelatinous to paste-like and, after drying, form an elastic film, for example, by addition of polvinyl alcohol, polyvinyl pyrrolidone, water-soluble cellulose derivatives or other more or less water-soluble film-forming agents. Microencapsulated substances can also be processed via the dispersion.

It is furthermore possible to apply membrane-forming substances separately in the production line, to accurately match the active ingredient, by including another screen printing unit without interfering with the adhesive.

If electron-beam cross-linking is to be carried out, this is advantageously effected after application of the adhesive and before application of the medicated active ingredient without interrupting the production line.

The coating is then advantageously dried in a hot-air canal or by infrared or high-frequency radiation.

Possible carrier webs are, in particular, diffusion-tight films. Particularly suitable carriers are those to which the adhesive and active ingredient formulation adhere without auxiliary materials. If appropriate, the surface of the carrier can also be additionally treated, for example, by corona discharge or coating with an adhesion promoter which, as a primer, effects anchoring of the active ingredient and adhesive elements.

A large number of medicinal active ingredients which are suitable for transdermal application are known. Thus, European Published Specification No. 72,251 describes a large number of such active ingredients. The following are examples:

Antihypertensive agents
Antihypotensive agents
Vasodilators
β-Blockers
Calcium antagonists
Antiemetic agents
Antitussive agents
Sedatives
Analgesics
Psychotropic agents
Antiasthmatic agents
Antirheumatic agents
Antiarythmic agents
Antihistamines
Hormones
Antibiotics
Cytostatics.

**4**

## BRIEF DESCRIPTION OF THE DRAWINGS

The features and advantages of the present invention will become more clearly appreciated from the following description taken in conjunction with the accompanying drawings in which:

FIG. 1 is a perspective view of one embodiment of the plaster of the present invention, and

FIG. 2 is a cross-sectional view of a second embodiment of the plaster of the present invention.

## DETAILED DESCRIPTION OF THE PREFERRED EMBODIMENTS

In FIG. 1, cap-shaped adhesive elements 2 and medicinal active ingredient elements 3 are located on a surface of a carrier web 1. A releasable cover 4 extends over the active ingredient and adhesive elements and is releasably retained by the adhesive elements. The cover 4 preferably has an adhesive-repellent finish on the side facing the adhesive elements 2 and active ingredient elements 3, if the cover 4 is not itself already adhesive-repellent.

FIG. 2 shows a variant of the FIG. 1 embodiment with the carrier web 1, adhesive composition elements 2 and active ingredient elements 3 embedded in an adhesive promoter 6 and covered with a releasable cover 4. On the underside of the carrier 1 is a covering lacquer 5 which can consist of a lacquer coating or a metal layer produced by vapor deposition.

The following is an example of a specific embodiment of the present invention:

### EXAMPLE

#### A.

#### Preparation of a medicated active ingredient formulation

27.35 parts by weight of hydroxypropylmethylcellulose (Pharmacoat 603) are stirred into a cold mixture of 30 parts by weight of isopropanol, 30 parts by weight of water and 8.20 parts by weight of 1,2-propylene glycol. The mixture is warmed to 50° C., with continuous stirring, until a clear solution has formed. 4.45 parts by weight of micronized 2-methyl-4-chloro-6-methoxy-5-(2-imidazoline-2-yl)-amino-pyrimidine (Moxonidin) are carefully mixed into said solution.

#### B.

#### Preparation of an adhesive formulation

100 parts by weight of a commercially available aqueous polymer dispersion based on acrylic acid ester (Acronal 80 D) are thickened to a viscosity of about 200 Pas by addition of 4 parts by weight of a 16% strength ammoniacal-aqueous solution of a polyacrylic acid (Collacral P).

#### C.

#### Printing Operation

A polyethylene terephthalate (Hostaphan RN 15) film 15 μm thick, which on one side is aluminized and lacquered the color of skin, is coated with the medicinal active ingredient formulation by a first rotating screen printing unit at a web speed of 20 m/minute. A perforated cylinder which produces rows of medicinal active ingredient elements in the longitudinal direction of the web is used. Each element has a base diameter of about 400 μm; the distance between the elements being about

4,699,792

**5**

100 μm in the longitudinal direction of the web and about 600 μm in the transverse direction. The amount applied is regulated via adjustment of the doctor blade so that cap-shaped elements are formed which, in the dried state, have a height of about 160 μm. This corresponds to about 25 g of medicated active ingredient formulation per m$^2$ of the carrier web. Drying is carried out at about 70° C. in a warm-air canal 6 m in length.

A second rotating screen printing unit of the same type then prints rows of elements of the adhesive formulation on the carrier web between the dried rows of elements containing the medicinal active ingredient. Thus, the amount of active ingredient formulation applied to a predetermined area of the carrier web is controlled by the element size and height. The second printing is followed by another drying zone of the type described above. The carrier web with the adhesive and medicated active ingredient elements is then passed through a laminating unit in which the web is covered with a releasable protective film, for example, a polyethylene terephthalate film 100 μm thick (Hostaphan RN 100), which is aluminized and siliconized on one side.

### D.

### Fabrication

The dried and covered web which has been printed twice is now divided into individual plasters of any desired size, depending on the desired doses of medicinal active ingredient. If, for example, a size of 25 cm$^3$ is chosen, this has in each case about 5000 elements of medicinal active ingredient and adhesive, the active ingredient content being about 7 mg of 2-methyl-4-chloro-6-methoxy-5-(2-imidazolin-2-yl)-amino-pyramidine (Moxonidin). These plasters are sealed individually in a diffusion-tight primary packing material, for example, a flat bag of polyethylene/aluminum/paper laminated material.

It will be appreciated that various arrangements of the above-disclosed arrangement are possible without departing from the spirit of the present invention.

What is claimed is:

1. A self-adhesive transdermal medicinal plaster in which the medication is isolated from the adhesive, comprising:
   (a) an impermeable carrier web;
   (b) a plurality of adhesive elements spaced from each other at predetermined locations on a surface of said carrier web; and
   (c) a plurality of active ingredient elements, containing at least one transdermal medication, spaced from each other and from said active ingredient elements at predetermined locations on said surface of said carrier web;
   (d) said active ingredient elements being disposed between a plurality of said adhesive elements and said adhesive elements being disposed between a plurality of said active ingredient elements on said surface of said carrier web, and the height of said active ingredient elements and the height of said adhesive elements on said carrier web being about the same to assure, when said plaster is applied to the skin, uniformly good contact of both said active ingredient and adhesive elements with the surface of the skin.

2. A self-adhesive medicinal plaster according to claim 5 wherein each of said adhesive elements and each of said medicinal active ingredient elements are

**6**

approximately cap-shaped and adhere at its base to said surface of said carrier web.

3. A self-adhesive medicinal plaster according to claim 2 wherein the apexes of said medicinal active ingredient elements and said adhesive elements are approximately the same height relative to said surface of said carrier web.

4. A self-adhesive medicinal plaster according to claim 5 wherein each of said medicinal active ingredient elements is surrounded by a plurality of said adhesive elements and each of said adhesive elements is surrounded by a plurality of said medicinal active ingredient elements.

5. A self-adhesive medicinal plaster according to claim 4 wherein said medicinal active ingredient elements and adhesive elements have a base dimension of up to about 5000 μm.

6. A self-adhesive medicinal plaster according to claim 5 wherein the base dimension of said medicinal active ingredient elements and said adhesive elements is between 200 and 1500 μm.

7. A self-adhesive medicinal plaster according to claim 5 wherein the adhesive of said adhesive elements is selected from the group consisting of rubber, a polyacrylic acid ester, polyisobutylene and mixtures thereof with tackifying resins.

8. A self-adhesive medicinal plaster according to claim 5 wherein said medicinal active ingredient further comprises at least one pharmaceutical auxiliary or excipient.

9. A self-adhesive medicinal plaster according to claim 5 further comprising an adhesion promoter coating on said surface of said carrier web for promoting adhesion of said medicinal active ingredient elements and said adhesive elements to said carrier web.

10. A self-adhesive medicinal plaster according to claim 5 further comprising a film covering the surface of said carrier web opposite said surface supporting said medicinal active ingredient and adhesive elements, said film being selected from the group consisting of lacquer and metal.

11. A self-adhesive medicinal plaster according to claim 5 wherein said active ingredient elements comprise 2-methyl-4-chloro-6-methoxy-5-(2-imidazolin-2-yl)-amino-pyramidine.

12. A self-adhesive medicinal plaster according to claim 5 wherein a portion of said active ingredient elements comprise one type of medicinal composition and the remainder of said active ingredient elements comprise a different medicinal composition.

13. A self-adhesive medicinal plaster according to claim 5 further comprising a releasable cover web covering said surface of said carrier web including said medicinal active ingredient and adhesive elements.

14. A method of making a self-adhesive transdermal medicinal plaster in which the medication is isolated from the adhesive, comprising applying, by gravure printing processes, a dispersion, plastisol or organisol of an adhesive having a high solids content and a dispersion of at least one transdermal medication having a high solids content at spaced locations on one surface of an impermeable carrier web and drying said adhesive and said medication to form a plurality of adhesive elements and a plurality of transdermal medicinal active ingredient elements spaced from each other at predetermined locations on said surface of said carrier web, said elements being arranged such that each of said medici-

4,699,792

7

8

nal active ingredient elements is disposed between a plurality of said adhesive elements and each of said adhesive elements is disposed between a plurality of said medicinal active ingredient elements, the amount of dispersion, plastisol or organisol of said adhesive and the amount of said dispersion of at least one medication applied to said carrier web being such that the height of the resultant adhesive elements and the height of the resultant active ingredient elements on said carrier web are about the same to assure, when said plaster is applied to skin, uniformly good contact of both said adhesive and active ingredient elements with the surface of the skin.

15. A method of making a self-adhesive plaster according to claim 19 wherein said gravure printing processes are screen printing processes.

16. A method of making a self-adhesive plaster according to claim 19 wherein said adhesive applied to said carrier web is an aqueous, thixotropic dispersion of adhesive with a solids content of 55–65% by weight.

17. A method of making a self-adhesive plaster according to claim 19 comprising first applying said adhesive to said carrier web, drying said adhesive to form said plurality of adhesive elements, and cross-linking the composition of said adhesive elements and then applying said medication to form said medicinal active ingredient elements and drying said medicated active ingredient elements.

18. A method of making a self-adhesive plaster according to claim 17 wherein said cross-linking of said adhesive elements is by means of electron beam radiation.

19. A method of making a self-adhesive plaster according to claim 14 wherein the amount of dispersion, plastisol or organisol of said adhesive and the amount of said dispersion of at least one medication applied by said gravure printing processes, respectively, provides adhesive elements and medicinal active ingredient elements respectively having a maximum base dimension of about 5000 $\mu$m.

20. A method of making a self-adhesive plaster according to claim 19 wherein said dispersion, plastisol or organisol of an adhesive having a high solids content is first applied by said gravure printing process to said surface of said carrier web and said adhesive is dried to form said plurality of adhesive elements on said carrier web and then said dispersion of at least one medication having a high solids content is applied by a further gravure printing process at spaced locations and spaced from said adhesive elements on said surface of said carrier web and said adhesive is dried to form said plurality of adhesive elements.

21. A method of making a self-adhesive plaster according to claim 19 wherein the amount of dispersion, plastisol or organisol of said adhesive and the amount of said dispersion of at least one medication applied by said gravure printing processes, respectively, provides adhesive elements and medicinal active ingredient elements respectivly having a base dimension between 200 and 1500 $\mu$m.

*  *  *  *  *

35

40

45

50

55

60

65

# United States Patent [19]

Edstrom et al.

[11] Patent Number: **Des. 316,225**

[45] Date of Patent: ∗∗ Apr. 16, 1991

[54] **BOTTLE**

[75] Inventors: **Richard C. Edstrom,** New York, N.Y.; **Richard N. Hirst,** Teaneck; **Richard B. Gerstman,** Tenafly, both of N.J.; **David O. Pressler,** Fairfield, Conn.

[73] Assignee: **Warner-Lambert Company,** Morris Plains, N.J.

[∗∗] Term: **14 Years**

[21] Appl. No.: **326,959**

[22] Filed: **Mar. 22, 1989**

[52] U.S. Cl. .................................................... **D9/404**

[58] Field of Search ............................. D9/403–413, D9/370; 215/1 R, 1 C

[56] **References Cited**

U.S. PATENT DOCUMENTS

D. 38,385 12/1906 Kohn ................................... D9/404
D. 94,157 12/1934 Marcus ................................ D9/404

D. 255,987 7/1980 Gentili ............................. D9/404
D. 262,778 1/1982 Britt et al. ......................... D9/404
D. 294,121 2/1988 Cramer ............................. D9/404

*Primary Examiner*—Melvin B. Feifer
*Assistant Examiner*—Lucy Lieberman
*Attorney, Agent, or Firm*—Charles A. Gaglia, Jr.

[57] **CLAIM**

The ornamental design for a bottle, as shown and described.

**DESCRIPTION**

FIG. 1 is a perspective view of a bottle showing our new design;

FIG. 2 is a top plan view thereof;

FIG. 3 is a side elevational view with the opposite side being identical;

FIG. 4 is a front elevational view with the rear elevation being identical; and

FIG. 5 is a bottom plan view.

The broken line showing of a bottle cap is for illustrative purposes only and forms no part of the claimed design.

THIS IS TO CERTIFY that this is a true copy from the records of the U.S. Patents and Trademark Office of the first page of the above identified patent:

Certifying Officer                    7/30/97

                                      Date

*FIG-1*

**U.S. Patent**     Apr. 16, 1991     Sheet 2 of 2     **Des. 316,225**

*FIG-2*

*FIG-3*

*FIG-4*

*FIG-5*

# FORM VA
**For a Work of the Visual Arts**
UNITED STATES COPYRIGHT OFFICE

REGISTRATION NUMBER

VA _____ VAU

EFFECTIVE DATE OF REGISTRATION

_____ _____ _____
Month      Day      Year

---

**DO NOT WRITE ABOVE THIS LINE. IF YOU NEED MORE SPACE, USE A SEPARATE CONTINUATION SHEET.**

## 1
**TITLE OF THIS WORK** ▼

**NATURE OF THIS WORK** ▼ See instructions

**PREVIOUS OR ALTERNATIVE TITLES** ▼

**PUBLICATION AS A CONTRIBUTION** If this work was published as a contribution to a periodical, serial, or collection, give information about the collective work in which the contribution appeared. **Title of Collective Work** ▼

If published in a periodical or serial give: **Volume** ▼      **Number** ▼      **Issue Date** ▼      **On Pages** ▼

## 2 a
**NAME OF AUTHOR** ▼

**DATES OF BIRTH AND DEATH**
Year Born ▼      Year Died ▼

Was this contribution to the work a "work made for hire"?
☐ Yes
☐ No

**AUTHOR'S NATIONALITY OR DOMICILE**
Name of Country
OR { Citizen of ▶ _____
Domiciled in ▶ _____

**WAS THIS AUTHOR'S CONTRIBUTION TO THE WORK**
Anonymous? ☐ Yes ☐ No
Pseudonymous? ☐ Yes ☐ No
If the answer to either of these questions is "Yes," see detailed instructions.

**NATURE OF AUTHORSHIP** Check appropriate box(es). **See instructions**
☐ 3-Dimensional sculpture
☐ 2-Dimensional artwork
☐ Reproduction of work of art
☐ Design on sheetlike material
☐ Map
☐ Photograph
☐ Jewelry design
☐ Technical drawing
☐ Text
☐ Architectural work

**NOTE**
Under the law, the "author" of a "work made for hire" is generally the employer, not the employee (see instructions). For any part of this work that was "made for hire" check "Yes" in the space provided, give the employer (or other person for whom the work was prepared) as "Author" of that part, and leave the space for dates of birth and death blank.

## b
**NAME OF AUTHOR** ▼

**DATES OF BIRTH AND DEATH**
Year Born ▼      Year Died ▼

Was this contribution to the work a "work made for hire"?
☐ Yes
☐ No

**AUTHOR'S NATIONALITY OR DOMICILE**
Name of Country
OR { Citizen of ▶ _____
Domiciled in ▶ _____

**WAS THIS AUTHOR'S CONTRIBUTION TO THE WORK**
Anonymous? ☐ Yes ☐ No
Pseudonymous? ☐ Yes ☐ No
If the answer to either of these questions is "Yes," see detailed instructions.

**NATURE OF AUTHORSHIP** Check appropriate box(es). **See instructions**
☐ 3-Dimensional sculpture
☐ 2-Dimensional artwork
☐ Reproduction of work of art
☐ Design on sheetlike material
☐ Map
☐ Photograph
☐ Jewelry design
☐ Technical drawing
☐ Text
☐ Architectural work

## 3 a
**YEAR IN WHICH CREATION OF THIS WORK WAS COMPLETED** This information must be given ◀ Year in all cases.

## b
**DATE AND NATION OF FIRST PUBLICATION OF THIS PARTICULAR WORK**
Complete this information ONLY if this work has been published.
Month ▶ _____ Day ▶ _____ Year ▶ _____
◀ Nation

## 4
**COPYRIGHT CLAIMANT(S)** Name and address must be given even if the claimant is the same as the author given in space 2. ▼

See instructions before completing this space.

**TRANSFER** If the claimant(s) named here in space 4 is (are) different from the author(s) named in space 2, give a brief statement of how the claimant(s) obtained ownership of the copyright. ▼

DO NOT WRITE HERE / OFFICE USE ONLY

APPLICATION RECEIVED

ONE DEPOSIT RECEIVED

TWO DEPOSITS RECEIVED

FUNDS RECEIVED

**MORE ON BACK ▶** • Complete all applicable spaces (numbers 5-9) on the reverse side of this page.
• See detailed instructions.      • Sign the form at line 8.

**DO NOT WRITE HERE**
Page 1 of _____ pages

| EXAMINED BY | FORM VA |
|---|---|
| CHECKED BY | |
| ☐ CORRESPONDENCE<br>Yes | FOR<br>COPYRIGHT<br>OFFICE<br>USE<br>ONLY |

**DO NOT WRITE ABOVE THIS LINE. IF YOU NEED MORE SPACE, USE A SEPARATE CONTINUATION SHEET.**

**5**

**PREVIOUS REGISTRATION** Has registration for this work, or for an earlier version of this work, already been made in the Copyright Office?
☐ Yes ☐ No If your answer is "Yes," why is another registration being sought? (Check appropriate box) ▼
a. ☐ This is the first published edition of a work previously registered in unpublished form.
b. ☐ This is the first application submitted by this author as copyright claimant.
c. ☐ This is a changed version of the work, as shown by space 6 on this application.
If your answer is "Yes," give: **Previous Registration Number** ▼          **Year of Registration** ▼

**6**

**DERIVATIVE WORK OR COMPILATION** Complete both space 6a and 6b for a derivative work; complete only 6b for a compilation.
a. **Preexisting Material** Identify any preexisting work or works that this work is based on or incorporates. ▼

See instructions
before completing
this space.

b. **Material Added to This Work** Give a brief, general statement of the material that has been added to this work and in which copyright is claimed. ▼

**7**

**DEPOSIT ACCOUNT** If the registration fee is to be charged to a Deposit Account established in the Copyright Office, give name and number of Account.
**Name** ▼          **Account Number** ▼

**CORRESPONDENCE** Give name and address to which correspondence about this application should be sent.   Name/Address/Apt/City/State/ZIP ▼

Be sure to
give your
◀ daytime phone
number

Area Code and Telephone Number ▶

**8**

**CERTIFICATION*** I, the undersigned, hereby certify that I am the
check only one ▼
☐ author
☐ other copyright claimant
☐ owner of exclusive right(s)
☐ authorized agent of _____
         Name of author or other copyright claimant, or owner of exclusive right(s) ▲

of the work identified in this application and that the statements made
by me in this application are correct to the best of my knowledge.

**Typed or printed name and date** ▼ If this application gives a date of publication in space 3, do not sign and submit it before that date.
                                                                    Date▶ _____

☞          Handwritten signature (X) ▼

**9**

**Mail
certificate
to:**

| Name ▼ |
|---|
| Number/Street/Apt ▼ |
| City/State/ZIP ▼ |

**Certificate
will be
mailed in
window
envelope**

**YOU MUST:**
• Complete all necessary spaces
• Sign your application in space 8
**SEND ALL 3 ELEMENTS
IN THE SAME PACKAGE:**
1. Application form
2. Nonrefundable $20 filing fee
   in check or money order
   payable to *Register of Copyrights*
3. Deposit material
**MAIL TO:**
Register of Copyrights
Library of Congress
Washington, D.C. 20559-6000

March 1995—300,000    ♲ PRINTED ON RECYCLED PAPER                    ☆U.S. GOVERNMENT PRINTING OFFICE: 1995–387-237/41

## TRADEMARK/SERVICE MARK APPLICATION, PRINCIPAL REGISTER, WITH DECLARATION

Mark (Identify the mark) _____ Class No. (If known) _____

Applicant Name: _____

Applicant Address: _____

Applicant Entity: (Check one and supply requested information)

☐ Individual—Citizenship (Country): _____

☐ Partnership—Partnership Domicile (State and Country): _____

Names and Citizenship (Country) of General Partners:_____

_____

☐ Corporation—State (Country, if appropriate) of Incorporation: _____

☐ Other (Specify Nature of Entity and Domicile): _____

To the Assistant Secretary and Commissioner of Patents and Trademarks:
Applicant requests registration of the above identified trademark/service mark shown in the accompanying drawing in the United States Patent and Trademark Office on the Principal Register established by the Act of July 5, 1946 (15 U.S.C. 1051 et seq., as amended) for the following goods/services: _____

_____

Basis for Application: (Check one or more, but not both the first and second boxes, and supply requested information)

☐ Applicant is using the mark in commerce on or in connection with the above identified goods/services. (15 U.S.C. 105(a), as amended.) Three specimens showing the mark as used in commerce are submitted with this application.

• Date of first use of the mark anywhere: _____

• Date of first use of the mark in commerce which the U.S. Congress may regulate: _____

• Specify the type of commerce (e.g., interstate, between the U.S. and a specified foreign country): _____

• Specify manner or mode of use of mark on or in connection with the goods/ services (e.g., trademark is applied to labels, service mark is used in advertisements): _____

☐ Applicant has bona fide intention to use the mark in commerce on or in connection with the above identified goods/services. (15 U.S.C. 105(b), as amended)

• Specify intended manner or mode of use of mark on or in connection with the goods or services (e.g., trademark will be applied to labels, service mark will be used in advertisements): _____

☐   Applicant has bona fide intention to use the mark in commerce on or in connection with the above identified goods/services, and asserts a claim of priority based upon a foreign application in accordance with (15 U.S.C. 1126(d), as amended).

Country of foreign filing: _____ Date of foreign filing: _____

☐   Applicant has a bona fide intention to use the mark in commerce on or in connection with the above identified goods/services and, accompanying this application, submits a certification or certified copy of a foreign registration in accordance with 15 U.S.C. 1126(e), as amended.

Country of registration: _____ Registration number: _____

## Declaration

The undersigned being hereby warned that willful false statements and the like so made are punishable by fine or imprisonment, or both, under 18 U.S.C. 1001, and that such willful false statements may jeopardize the validity of the application or any resulting registration, declares that he/she is properly authorized to execute this application on behalf of the applicant; he/she believes the applicant to be the owner of the trademark/service mark sought to be registered or, if the application is being filed under 15 U.S.C. 105(b), he/she believes applicant to be entitled to use such mark in commerce; to the best of his/her knowledge and belief no other person, firm, corporation, or association has the right to use the above identified mark in commerce, either in the identical form thereof or in such near resemblance thereto as to be likely, when used on or in connection with the goods/services of such other person; to cause confusion, or to cause mistake, or to deceive; and that all statements made of his/her own knowledge are true and all statements made on information and belief are believed to be true.

_____        _____
SIGNATURE                               DATE

_____        _____
PRINT OR TYPE NAME AND POSITION         TELEPHONE

# CHAPTER 3

# Finding Help in Protecting and Marketing Inventions

Protecting and profiting from your ideas and inventions is no easy exercise, as a considerable amount of time, money, effort, and networking is required. No matter what your skills and experience level, you will likely need assistance in making your ideas a success. Whether this source of assistance is from patent attorneys and agents, invention brokers and promotion firms, inventor's clubs, or universities, please ensure that you are dealing with reputable people and organizations.

## Patent Attorneys and Agents

There are numerous resources to help you protect and market your ideas and inventions. Patent attorneys and agents have already been mentioned as sources of assistance in conducting patent searches and filing and prosecuting patent applications. Patent attorneys can also be helpful in licensing your invention and in enforcing your intellectual property rights.

The PTO has geographical and alphabetical listings of patent attorneys and agents, but it does not make recommendations or assume responsibility for your selection from the lists. You can also find patent attorneys and agents by looking in the classified section of your telephone directory under the heading Patent Attorneys.

Typical attorney's fees for preparing and filing a patent application for a simple idea or invention range from about $3,000 to $5,000. Typical fees for prosecuting applications in the PTO are approximately $5,000 to $10,000. Chapter 5 of this book provides additional information on using patent attorneys and agents.

## Invention Promoters and Brokers

Invention promotion firms are another resource to help you protect and profit from your ideas and inventions. These firms will take on a part of the job or the entire job of protecting, developing, and marketing your idea. They can typically be found in the telephone directory listed under the headings Patents, Inventions, or Invention Promotion. Some firms are also advertised on late-night television.

Always exercise caution when doing business with invention promotion firms. These firms typically charge fees from $1,000 to $10,000, and they may not have a proven track record of success. In fact, many firms are sham operations that prey on unsuspecting inventors. These unethical invention promoters will typically glorify all ideas, charge a large up-front fee, and do little or nothing with the ideas. Several firms have been fined and penalized by state and federal governments and were the subject of congressional hearings.

If you elect to use an invention promotion firm, choose one that (1) can provide solid evidence of its track record—not just a few flashy success stories, but verifiable statistics on the number of clients it has had and the number who have actually made money; (2) does not collect the entire fee in advance; and (3) will provide samples of its promotional materials and lists of companies to whom it has sent it; then check with those companies yourself. Check the promotion firm's reputation with the state attorney general, Better Business Bureau, Chamber of Commerce, patent attorney, local inventors or innovator's club, or with former clients of the firm.

Invention brokers can also be helpful in making your invention a success. Invention brokers typically work for a portion of the profits from the invention and their initial fees are relatively small. You can find invention brokers through listings in the telephone directory or through inventor's clubs, patent attorneys, or your local library.

Invention brokers may help raise money and form companies or strategic alliances to produce and market your inventions. They often provide management research and development advice. In general, brokers are interested in relatively complex technology with a fairly large sales potential.

Only do business with reputable invention promotion or broker firms. Make sure you investigate the firms and fully understand what services are provided and what financial obligations are required of you. Be certain that all of the terms are stated in a written agreement.

Some noted firms that work with promising inventors and small companies across the country are:

- The Battelle Memorial Institute, Invention Administrator, 505 King Avenue, Columbus, OH 43201; (614) 424-6424
- Arthur D. Little Enterprises, Invention Management Department, Acorn Park, Cambridge, MA 02140-2390; (617) 864-5770
- Product Resources International, 1414 Avenue of the Americas, New York, NY 10168; (212) 687-4741
- REFAC Technology Development Corporation, 122 E. Forty-second Street, New York, NY 10017; (212) 687-4741

Refer to chapter 4 of this book for additional information on using invention brokers and promotion firms.

## Inventor's Clubs, Associations and Societies

Inventor's clubs, associations, and societies may be located in your region. Opportunities for professional, business, and social networking are often provided by inventor's organizations. These centers of innovation can be valuable sources of information and services. For their locations, contact the following organizations:

- United Inventors Association of the United States of America (UIA-USA), P.O. Box 50305, St. Louis, MO 63105 *(stamped, self-addressed envelope required)*
- National Congress of Inventor Organizations (NCIO), 727 North 600 West, Logan, UT 84321; (801) 753-0888

One group, the Inventors Awareness Group Inc., provides a network of information for inventors. This group is located at 171 Interstate Drive, Suite 6, West Springfield, MA 01089-4533. The National Congress of Inventor Organizations provides similar information (see above). Local organizations such as The Minnesota Inventors Congress (P.O. Box 71, Redwood, MN 56283; 800/468-3681) assist inventors seeking connection with business, educational, and promotional resources. Contact the inventor's organizations in your area.

Talking with other inventors can be very helpful. Find another inventor who has already filed a patent, applied research and development, and experienced the stages of financing. It does not matter if his or her end result was a financial success or failure. Getting the nuts and bolts of the process can be helpful to you.

Bounce your ideas, in confidence, off other inventors. Welcome their criticism, and do not be afraid to ask for their assistance in finding ways to perfect, patent, and market your ideas.

## University Invention and Entrepreneurial Centers

Invention and entrepreneurial centers operated by universities and the National Science Foundation can be valuable sources of help with your ideas and inventions. The University of Oregon's Experimental Center for the Advancement of Invention and Innovation, for example, evaluates ideas for a modest fee.

Invention and entrepreneurial centers can help inventors weed out bad ideas so they will not waste further time and money. The centers can also identify trouble spots that require special attention in planning the development or commercialization of a potential new product. If an idea shows it has merit and is commercially feasible, the centers try to link the inventor with established companies or refer him or her to sources of funds. Similar programs may be available at colleges and universities in your area.

## The Small Business Administration

The Small Business Administration (SBA) operates Small Business Institutes (SBI) located at several hundred colleges and universities throughout the country. Currently, few SBI centers can provide much help with the technical research and development aspects of innovations, although they may be able to provide the necessary assistance in market research, feasibility analysis, and business planning to make an invention successful.

Small Business Administration field offices (listed in your local telephone directory under the heading U.S. Government) can provide information about the SBI program. You may find other management assistance programs offered at the field offices that can be helpful in developing your idea as well. Publications containing information on patenting and marketing inventions are available by writing to the Small Business Administration, 1441 L Street, NW, Washington, D.C. 20416 (800/827-5722).

## National Bureau of Standards

The Office of Energy-Related Inventions in the U.S. Department of Commerce's National Bureau of Standards sometimes evaluates, free of charge, nonnuclear energy-related inventions and ideas for devices, materials, and procedures. If the office finds that the invention or idea has merit, it can recommend further study by the Department of Energy, which may provide support for the invention if they believe it shows promise.

This process can take up to a year, but it could be fruitful for energy-related inventions. For further information on this program, write to the U.S. Department of Commerce, Office of Energy-Related Inventions, Washington, D.C. 20230 or the U.S. Department of Energy, Office of Technical and Financial Assistance, Washington, D.C. 20585.

## Manufacturers and Distributors

Often you can go directly to prospective manufacturers and distributors, particularly small to medium-sized firms, for assistance in commercializing your ideas. Be certain to take the required steps to protect your idea by a patent, copyright, trademark, confidentiality agreement, or otherwise. Check the telephone directory and the library for listings of potential manufacturers. Compile a list of local, national, and international manufacturers who might be interested in manufacturing and distributing your product.

Check local and national trade publications in the field of your invention, as well as sources such as *Moody's*, *Standard & Poor's*, *Dun's Million Dollar Directory*, and the *Thomas Register*. Some retailers, such as Kmart, J. C. Penney, Hammacher Schlemmer, Sharper Image, and others, may welcome new ideas and may assist in developing and marketing them. Most large companies are not favorable to outside ideas for fear of litigation.

Some companies will require that you sign a waiver before they accept submission of your idea. This waiver typically provides that the company has no obligations to maintain your idea in confidence or to compensate you if they use your idea. If your idea is patented, or will be patented or otherwise protected by intellectual property rights, this waiver is less of a concern. Nevertheless, avoid signing such a waiver if possible. Rather, ask the companies to sign your confidentiality agreement. If you have friends or contacts at these companies, use them to your advantage in making introductions to key decision makers.

Prepare a professional model or portfolio of your idea. If you work with a model maker or other artisan, enter into a contract for services that acknowledges your ownership of the idea and any improvements and that obligates the contractor to confidentiality. Demonstrate your model or show the portfolio of your idea to prospective manufacturers and distributors. Keep your presentation simple, yet professional.

Be prepared to explain the function, operation, benefits, and perceived market of your invention and understand the anticipated costs, competition, and business risks. Show how your idea fits with the manufacturer's existing or future lines of products and services.

Talk to a number of manufacturers at the same time. See if you can generate interest at several companies, and go with the company that offers the greatest potential. Evaluate the companies just as they are evaluating you and your idea. Ask to see their new product catalogs and bulletins. Check the reputations of the companies with the Better Business Bureau and consumer affairs agencies.

Try to deal directly with the people who are in a position to make decisions regarding your idea. Focus your efforts on the presidents of the companies, directors of research and development, and others in charge of intellectual property or invention submissions.

Be willing to discuss what you want out of the deal. Do you want to sell the invention or license it? Are you interested in being involved in the manufacturing or marketing of your invention? What would be an acceptable sales price or royalty rate for your invention?

After you have reached an agreement with a manufacturer or distributor, present the terms in a written contract and have it signed by you and an authorized representative of the company. You should probably have a patent or licensing attorney assist you in the negotiations or review the agreement before you sign it. Additional information on licensing your inventions is provided in chapter 12.

# CHAPTER 4

# Dealing with Invention Brokers and Promotion Firms

ANY INVENTORS TURN to invention brokers or invention promotion firms for help in commercializing their inventions. Some of the reputable firms with a proven track record may help you get your idea or invention into the marketplace. Inventors anxious to get their products to market, however, are routinely taken advantage of by unscrupulous invention promotion firms that steal their ideas or neglect to promote the invention after collecting large fees from the inventors.

Distinguishing between a fraudulent invention promotion firm and a legitimate one is often difficult. Unscrupulous and honest firms use similar advertising and sales techniques, market evaluations, and contract strategies. You need to know how to spot common signs of trouble, how to protect yourself, and what to do if you become a victim.

## Evaluating Invention Promoters

There are legitimate invention promotion firms as well as many disreputable ones. As an aspiring inventor, you need to be able to tell the good firms from the bad firms. Investigating and evaluating the reputation and track record of each firm is the first step in protecting yourself.

Many government agencies and private organizations offer information and assistance to independent inventors in dealing with invention marketing and promotion firms. These agencies and organizations include the PTO, the SBA, the FTC, and inventor's clubs and associations. The FTC is particularly aggressive in monitoring and policing the activities of invention promoters and offers these helpful points in comparing legitimate and illegitimate firms.

Examine the advertising and sales techniques of each firm for false, misleading, and impractical claims. Some invention promotion firms advertise in classified ads in newspapers and magazines and through television and radio. They target independent inventors and frequently offer free information to help patent and market inventions. These firms may also advertise a toll-free telephone number that inventors can call for written information. The information, however, usually consists only of brochures about the promoter.

If you respond to the ads, a salesperson may contact you and will likely request information about you, your idea, and a sketch of the invention. As an inducement, the firm may offer a free preliminary review of your invention.

Some invention promotion firms may claim to know or have special access to manufacturers who are likely to be interested in licensing your invention. These kinds of claims often can be false or exaggerated. Be cautious of firms that claim to have special access to independent manufacturers, especially when they refuse to document such claims. Therefore, before signing a contract with an invention promotion firm that claims special relationships with particular manufacturers, ask for proof to support its claims.

After a preliminary review of your invention, a firm might request a market evaluation on your idea, which may cost several hundred dollars. Such evaluations from questionable firms often make vague and general statements and provide no hard evidence that there is a market for your invention. Reputable companies report specific information. Before you pay for a report on your idea, ask what specific information you will receive and demand that it be put in writing.

## Checklist for Using Invention Promoters

If you are interested in working with an invention promotion firm, follow the checklist below before you sign a contract and pay significant amounts of money.

- Early in your discussions with a promotion firm, ask what the total cost of its services will be. Be warned if the salesperson hesitates to answer.
- Be careful of an invention promotion firm that offers to review or evaluate your invention but refuses to disclose details concerning its criteria, system of review, and qualifications of company evaluators. Without this information, you cannot assess the competence of the firm or make meaningful comparisons with other firms. Reputable firms should provide an objective evaluation of the merit, technical feasibility, and commercial viability of your invention.
- Require the firm to check existing invention patents. Because unscrupulous firms are willing to promote virtually any idea or invention with no regard to its patentability, they may unwittingly promote an idea for which someone already has a valid, unexpired patent. This means that even if the promotional efforts of your invention are successful, you may find yourself the subject of a patent infringement lawsuit. If no valid, unexpired patent exists for your idea, seek advice from a patent professional before authorizing the public disclosure of your idea.
- Be wary of an invention promotion firm that will not disclose its rates of success and rejection. Success rates show the number of clients who made more money from their invention than they paid to the firm. Rejection rates reflect the percentage of all ideas or inventions that was found unacceptable by the

invention promotion company. Check with your state and local consumer protection officials to learn if invention promotion firms are required to disclose their rates of success and rejection in your locality.

In reality, few inventions make it to the marketplace and still fewer become commercial successes. According to experts used in FTC cases, an invention promotion firm that does not reject most of the inventions it reviews may be unduly optimistic, if not dishonest, in its evaluations.

- Be wary of a firm that claims to have special access to manufacturers looking for new products but refuses to document such claims. Legitimate invention promotion firms substantiate their claims.

- Be skeptical of claims and assurances that your invention will make money. No one can guarantee the success of your invention.

- Avoid being taken in solely on a firm's promotional brochures and affiliations with organizations that appear impressive. Beware of high-pressure sales tactics.

- Investigate the company before making any commitments. Call the Better Business Bureau, consumer protection agency, and attorney general in your state and in the state where the company is located to learn if they know of any unresolved consumer complaints about the firm.

- Make sure your contract contains all agreed upon terms, written and verbal, before you sign. The contract should specify that the invention promoter will perform significant services such as identifying prospective manufacturers, preparing an invention presentation or demonstration, building and testing the invention, and negotiating a license or sales agreement for you. Make sure the agreement sets a time limit for the invention promoter to succeed. If possible, have an attorney review the agreement.

- If you do not get satisfactory answers to all your questions with an invention promotion firm, consider whether you want to sign a contract. Once a dishonest company has your money, it is unlikely your money will be returned.

- If you believe you are a victim of a fraudulent invention

promotion firm, contact the firm immediately and ask for your money back. If the firm does not return your money, report your problem to the Better Business Bureau, local consumer protection agency, and the attorney general in your state and in the state where the company is located. Your information may help an ongoing investigation or demonstrate the need for one.

You also may file a complaint by writing to the FTC. The FTC generally does not intervene in individual disputes; however, the information you provide may indicate a pattern of possible law violations.

The addresses and telephone numbers for the national and regional offices of the FTC are listed below.

### FTC Headquarters

6th & Pennsylvania Avenue, NW, Washington, D.C. 20580; (202) 326-2222

### FTC Regional Offices

- 1718 Peachtree Street, NW, Suite 1000, Atlanta, GA 30367; (404) 347-4836
- 101 Merrimac Street, Suite 810, Boston, MA 02114-4719; (617) 424-5960
- 55 East Monroe Street, Suite 1437, Chicago, IL 60603; (312) 353-4423
- 668 Euclid Avenue, Suite 520-A, Cleveland, OH 44114; (216) 522-4207
- 100 North Central Expressway, Suite 500, Dallas, TX 75201; (214) 767-5501
- 1504 Curtis Street, Suite 2900, Denver, CO 80202-2393; (303) 844-2271
- 11000 Wilshire Boulevard, Suite 13209, Los Angeles, CA 90024; (310) 575-7575
- 150 William Street, Suite 1300, New York, NY 10038; (212) 264-1207
- 901 Market Street, Suite 570, San Francisco, CA 94103; (415) 744-7920
- 2806 Federal Building, 915 Second Avenue, Seattle, WA 98174; (206) 220-6363

# CHAPTER 5

# Using Patent Attorneys and Patent Agents

I F AN INVENTION is to receive patent protection in the United States, a patent application must be written to describe and claim the invention and must be filed and prosecuted to allowance with the PTO. Although many inventors have successfully drafted their own patent applications, many others have hired either a patent agent or a patent attorney to draft and prosecute the application. This chapter provides guidance on how to select a patent agent or a patent attorney and how to work most efficiently and effectively with your agent or attorney to obtain the best possible patent protection at a reasonable cost. Remember that patent attorneys and patent agents can also provide assistance in conducting literature searches and reviewing the prior art to determine if your invention is patentable. Patent attorneys can help in licensing your invention and enforcing your patent against infringers.

## Who Can Represent You in Patent Matters

An inventor can be represented before the PTO by himself or herself or a registered patent agent or patent attorney. There are advantages and disadvantages to representing yourself or using a patent attorney or patent agent. Many factors should be considered in deciding your representation.

Preparing an application for patent and conducting the proceedings in the PTO to obtain the patent is an undertaking that requires knowledge of patent law and practices of the PTO. Knowledge of the scientific or technical matters involved in the particular invention are also required. Inventors may prepare their own applications, file them in the PTO, and conduct the proceedings, but they may face considerable difficulty unless they are familiar with these matters or study them in detail. While a patent may be obtained, in many cases, by persons not skilled in this work, there would be no assurance that the obtained patent would adequately protect the invention.

On the other hand, the inventor who originated the idea for which patent protection is sought knows the idea better than anyone else. Drafting a patent application based on that idea is usually within the grasp of an inventor who is comfortable with drafting technical papers. Many inventors write their own patent applications, although caution is advised. Patent laws are complex, and knowledge of them can mean the difference between obtaining a patent that adequately protects the invention and failing to receive any patent protection at all. Thus, even if the inventor writes the application, it makes good sense to retain a patent agent or patent attorney to review the draft. Instructions for writing a patent application are provided later in this book.

Many inventors employ the services of registered patent attorneys or patent agents. By law, the PTO has the power to make rules and regulations that govern the conduct of patent attorneys and agents and recognize attorneys and agents who are qualified to practice before the PTO. Persons who are not recognized for this practice are not permitted by law to represent inventors before the PTO. The PTO maintains a register of attorneys and agents. To be admitted to this register, a person must comply with the regulations prescribed by the office, which require a showing that the person is of good moral character and good repute and that he or she has the legal, scientific, and technical qualifications necessary to render a valuable service to patent applicants. These qualifications must be demonstrated by passing an examination.

Admission to practice in and represent clients before the PTO has been granted to two classes of people: patent agents and patent attorneys. The basic qualifications of both classes are the same. The prospective agent or attorney must have sufficient technical knowledge to understand the ideas brought to him or her by inventors and to describe and discuss those ideas adequately. Possession of a bachelor of science (B.S.) in the engineering disciplines, such as electrical engineering, mechanical engineering, or chemical engineering, or in the sciences, such as physics, chemistry, or biology, is sufficient technical background. For applicants who do not have a degree in these or similar areas, the PTO evaluates the applicant's technical course work to determine if the applicant can successfully represent clients.

The major difference between patent agents and patent attorneys is that agents usually do not have a law degree and are, consequently, not lawyers. Although agents have the basic minimum knowledge of the patent law required by the PTO, they are not trained in general legal matters and cannot represent an inventor in a court or jurisdiction other than the PTO. Insofar as preparing an application for patent and conducting the prosecution in the PTO, patent agents are usually just as well qualified as patent attorneys. Patent agents cannot conduct patent litigation in the courts or perform various services that the local jurisdiction considers as practicing law. For example, a patent agent could not draw up a contract relating to a patent, such as an assignment or a license, if the state in which he or she resides considers drawing contracts as practicing law.

The PTO cannot recommend any particular attorney or agent, or aid in the selection of an attorney or agent, as by stating, in response to inquiry, that a named patent attorney, agent, or firm is "reliable" or "capable." There is a directory, published by the PTO that lists all registered patent attorneys and agents who have indicated availability to accept new clients. The directory is arranged by states, cities, and countries and can be purchased from the U.S. Government Printing Office (GPO).

The classified section or Yellow Pages in telephone directories of most large cities have a heading for patent attorneys under which those in that area are listed. Many large cities also have associations of patent attorneys, which may be helpful in finding an appropriate patent attorney or agent.

In employing a patent attorney or agent, the inventor executes a power of attorney or authorization to the agent. The power of attorney is usually part of the application papers and is filed in the PTO. When an attorney has been appointed, the PTO does not communicate with the inventor directly but conducts correspondence with the attorney who is acting for the inventor. The inventor is free to contact the PTO concerning the status of his or her application. The inventor may remove the attorney or agent by revoking the power of attorney at any time.

## Choosing Between Patent Agents and Patent Attorneys

If the inventor has decided not to draft a patent application on his or her own, then the inventor must choose between retaining a patent agent or a patent attorney. The choice is not clear-cut and either may be perfectly acceptable in a given situation. Several factors should be considered in making the decision.

By far the most important factor from the inventor's point of view is the ability of the prospective agent or attorney to understand the invention, to describe it well in a patent application, and to prosecute it to allowance with the PTO.

The level of technical expertise required from the patent agent or attorney can vary widely. Simple mechanical or electrical inventions may be readily understood by anyone with a minimal amount of technical knowledge. Innovative computer architectures and new monoclonal antibodies may require a Ph.D. in electrical engineering or biochemistry, respectively. The inventor should exercise a great deal of self-honesty in evaluating the invention and appraising the amount of technical knowledge needed to understand it. Although even the simplest invention can be incredibly useful and profitable, hiring a patent agent or attorney with technical qualifications greater than necessary will undoubtedly cost the inventor more money in legal fees. Whether an agent or attorney, a person with a Ph.D. will likely charge more than one with a B.S. By honestly appraising the technical complexity of one's own invention and by hiring an agent or attorney with an adequate technical knowledge necessary to understand the invention, the inventor can obtain more cost-effective representation.

The technical complexity of the invention can also affect the potential legal complexity of the case, and the legal complexity is another factor to consider in choosing between an agent and an attorney. Although patent agents have much experience in drafting and prosecuting patent applications on highly complex technology, they typically do not have any experience in negotiating and drafting patent licenses or in patent litigation, except perhaps as an advisor. In general, you will pay significantly less in legal fees if you use a patent agent instead of a patent attorney. Once again, you can save money by honestly appraising the legal complexity of the invention and by hiring a patent agent or attorney based on your needs. If commercialization is a possibility for your invention, and if there is a high likelihood of copying by third parties and potential litigation, it may be beneficial to hire a patent attorney with litigation experience to draft and prosecute the application, as opposed to an agent with no such experience.

In selecting a patent agent or attorney, the inventor should conduct a background evaluation. Make sure that the agent or attorney is registered with the PTO. Ask each potential agent or attorney to provide samples of granted U.S. patents that he or she has drafted and prosecuted, preferably in the field of your idea. Read these patents carefully and determine if the agent or attorney can write clearly about the relevant technology. The patents should be clear, complete, and easy to understand. Although the claims section of every patent must be written in a precise and legally prescribed manner, a good set of claims should still be understandable even to a relatively inexperienced inventor. If the patents seem unnecessarily long or difficult to read, discuss this with the agent or attorney and consider this a factor in making a selection.

Every patent agent or attorney should be willing to provide a list of references who can be called to discuss their experiences in working with the agent or attorney. Ask the agent or attorney for a list of references and call several of the references to investigate the agent's or attorney's reputation. Appropriate questions to ask include: Did the agent/attorney take a reasonable amount of time to understand the invention? Did the agent/attorney set a schedule for completing the application and was that schedule kept? Did the agent/attorney communicate well at all stages of the preparation and prosecution of the application? When investigating an attorney, the inventor should also contact the state bar to which the attorney is admitted to determine whether the attorney has previous or pending disciplinary actions against him or her. There are simply too many qualified patent agents and attorneys available to retain one whom others have found difficult to work with or who is of questionable character.

Other factors that should be considered in selecting an agent or attorney are location, access, and convenience. All other factors being equal, a local agent or attorney with whom face to face meetings are easy to arrange and attend is preferable to an attorney or agent located far away. Location used to be a greater problem when finding patent agents and attorneys outside of Washington, D.C., and other major urban areas was difficult. However, finding competent local patent agents and attorneys is no longer difficult in most parts of the country.

Another factor in selecting between a patent agent and attorney is the marketability of the invention. The more assistance the inventor believes he or she will need to market or license the invention, the more attention should be paid to the business experience of the patent agent or attorney. Even if an attorney does not have an extensive business law practice, he or she will probably have seen many more patent licenses and confidential disclosure agreements than an agent.

Always remember that you are not locked into any one form of representation. It is easy to imagine circumstances where a patent agent is selected to draft the patent application and prosecute it, but a patent attorney is later retained when the prosecution becomes more complex than originally anticipated. Similarly, the agent may bring the invention through the entire patent application process, at which point a patent attorney is retained to help license and market the invention.

## Selecting Cost-Effective Representation

Patent agents and attorneys operate under a variety of arrangements and fee schedules, and you should always select the ones that will provide the most cost-effective representation. Although patent agents can share office space, they cannot form professional corporations. Even though some agents are employed by law firms, the choice of hiring an agent will be based on the personal qualifications of the individual patent agent. Patent attorneys, on the other hand, may practice alone or in professional corporations or in law firms consisting of any number of attorneys. Within a firm, there are typically two classes of attorneys: partners, who actually own shares of the professional corporation, and associates, who are employees of the firm but not shareholders. The first choice for an inventor is often whether to retain an attorney or agent practicing on his or her own or to retain a law firm; there are no fixed rules for making this choice.

Many competent patent attorneys have found the legal practice within a firm unacceptable and have decided to pursue their careers as solo practitioners. They are usually free to work whatever hours they choose; do not have a yearly minimum billable hours requirement, as associates and partners in firms typically have; and are free to establish any type of fee relationship with their clients that they wish based on their individual financial situations. A few years ago, establishing a solo practice was an expensive proposition. An office was typically rented, secretarial help and bookkeeping assistance hired, and a professional library purchased or leased. Even with the development of shared office arrangements in recent years where several solo practitioners shared the aforementioned services and facilities, the fixed costs were relatively high and these were reflected in the charge structure that solo practitioners offered.

Because of the development of powerful and relatively inexpensive computers, with inexpensive and powerful software for word processing, accounting, and docketing, along with Internet access to various legal databases and research services, the costs of establishing a solo patent practice are now relatively small. With these developments, many talented patent agents and attorneys have established solo practices with highly competitive rates. Thus, an inventor who retains a solo practitioner can often get a more personal and cost-effective service than an inventor who retains the services of a large law firm.

There are a few disadvantages to retaining a solo practitioner. Most importantly, if the solo agent or attorney experiences an illness, accident, or emergency, he or she may suddenly be un-available. Although many attorneys have arrangements for such emergency situations, a situation can still occur where the carefully chosen attorney is suddenly not available, and an unknown attorney provides the service instead.

The solo patent attorney also may not be able to readily consult with another patent attorney, should the preparation of the appli-cation involve a technology that is unfamiliar to the attorney or should the prosecution of the application generate a new and unforeseen legal twist that the attorney has not handled before. The informal consultation and exchange of ideas that occurs in law firms often adds a great deal of value, even if it occurs in a manner unseen by most clients.

Patent law firms can range from two to more than one hundred attorneys, with larger law firms frequently having satellite offices in other cities and, in some cases, other countries. While there are many firms that specialize in only the practice of patent and intellectual property law, other law firms consist of attorneys who practice in many different legal areas, such as corporate law, antitrust, and mergers and acquisitions, with only a few patent attorneys within the firm forming a "patent boutique." These patent boutiques may share some of the disadvantages of solo practice, where the patent attorney does not necessarily have colleagues to discuss patent issues with. Further, patent boutiques may also share some of the disadvantages of practice in a large firm such as high overhead costs and resultant high hourly rates.

Choosing among the array of patent agents, patent attorneys, and law firms is not a simple task. Consequently, insist on meeting both the billing partner as well as the associate who will draft the case. The factors that were mentioned earlier in choosing between a patent agent and a patent attorney (e.g., technical competence, legal experience, costs, and personal rapport) should also be applied in making a choice between a solo attorney and a law firm.

Regardless of the level of complexity of the invention, expect that the attorney with whom you will be working will have a good general knowledge of the relevant area of technology. Although you will have to explain the details of the invention to the attorney, you should not have to pay for a technical review course for the attorney. Remember that competence in subject matter can be established several ways, such as the educational background of the attorney and previous patent experience in the particular technology as evidenced by issued patents on similar matters.

The legal fee is perhaps the most difficult issue discussed with the prospective attorney. Discuss this issue fully and obtain a written fee arrangement before beginning any substantive work. Many types of fee arrangements are possible, and they should all be explored before a final fee agreement is reached. Exercise great care in this area, as misunderstanding and disagreement about fees results in unnecessary and undesirable litigation between clients and their former attorneys.

In patent law practice, the two primary fee structures are an hourly rate and a set fee for a designated service. Historically, attorney services were billed by the hour, and this practice remains common today. But, increasingly small independent inventors and solo practitioners are using the set fee for service arrangement. With the set fee arrangement, the inventor and attorney generally review the case and then the attorney proposes a single fee for handling the matter.

Both fee structures may be workable, but the most cost-effective arrangement should be pursued. If a fixed fee is used, the agreement might contain a provision that permits an additional sum if more time and work by the attorney is needed than initially anticipated by the inventor and the attorney. If an hourly rate is used, an estimate of the time to complete the patent application or other work should be obtained from the attorney. The inventor should be contacted for approval if more time is required than what was documented in the estimate. Again, no work should be started until both the inventor and the attorney have reached an acceptable fee arrangement and have put that fee arrangement into a written agreement.

When working with a law firm, understand that the partners and associates typically have different hourly rates. If an associate is going to handle a patent matter, ensure that only a reasonable amount of additional time is spent by the partner to review the associate's work. Know the billing rate of each attorney who might work on your case before he or she begins.

It is difficult to state which patent agent, attorney or law firm will provide the best rate for preparing and prosecuting a patent application or handling other patent work. Because the fixed costs of a solo patent agent or solo attorney are somewhat lower than those of most firms, the individual agent or attorney can frequently perform patent work at a very competitive rate. Solo practitioners are typically more willing to perform work, such as drafting a patent application, for a fixed fee than are many law firms. However, some law firms see patent prosecution as a "loss leader" and are willing to provide patent preparation and prosecution services at a rate well below their normal fees to gain a position for the client's future licensing and litigation work.

Ask for a listing of all likely additional charges such as copying costs, telephone charges, travel expenses. Fees from the PTO should also be factored into the final cost estimate. As with any other good or service, shopping around for legal services is the best way to determine their relative cost-effectiveness.

## The Initial Meeting Between Inventor and Patent Attorney

Once a you have retained a patent agent or attorney, he or she can review the invention for patentability and prepare and prosecute a U.S. patent application. The process usually starts with an initial meeting between the inventor and the agent or attorney to review the merits of the invention. Careful planning for the initial meeting can expedite the preparation of a good patent application and lay the groundwork for an expeditious prosecution and allowance of the application. At the initial meeting with the patent attorney or agent, bring all the information and materials necessary to give him or her a clear understanding of your invention.

Determining whether the invention is patentable requires a review of what inventions already exist in the relevant technical field. Conducting a prior art search is the best way to learn about earlier patents and publications. Although it is possible to prepare and file a patent application without conducting a prior art search, this generally results in an unfocused application, as the invention will not be presented in the context of related existing technology. This could also result in a situation where the PTO rejects the application based on a number of references having every feature of the invention. It is also quite possible that the prior art search conducted by the PTO as part of the patent application examination process will not find the most relevant prior art to the invention; this could result in a patent that is easily invalidated. The risks of not performing any prior art search before drafting and filing the patent application outweigh the relatively small, incremental cost of having the attorney or agent perform at least a basic prior art search.

Provide the attorney or agent with copies of all relevant prior art of which you are aware. This will aid him or her with the patentability review, preparation of the patent application, and compliance with the duty to disclose to the PTO all relevant prior art that is known by you, the inventor, and those assisting with the patent application.

Provide the patent agent or attorney with all drawings and figures, including flow charts, that aid in understanding the assembly or operation of your invention. At some point during the prosecution of the application, the drawings must be revised to meet requirements of the PTO. Informal drawings may be submitted if they fulfill the minimal requirement of allowing the reader of the application to re-create the invention and show all features for which the inventor is claiming patent protection. By filing the application with informal drawings, it is possible to delay the expense of creating formal drawings until the PTO decides to allow the application.

Having received an explanation of the invention and all relevant material, the attorney or agent will carefully review the materials for complete understanding of how the invention operates. The results of the prior art search will also be reviewed so both the inventor and attorney or agent can determine differences between the prior art references and the invention.

## Using the Sample Attorney Retainer Agreement

A sample Attorney Retainer Agreement is provided at the end of this chapter for use when hiring a patent agent or patent attorney. Any time you hire an agent or attorney, a written agreement should be entered into to clearly spell out the rights and responsibilities of each party.

The sample agreement includes the date, the name and address of the client, and the name and office address of the attorney or agent. The agreement should describe, as completely as possible, the transaction or matter for which legal representation is sought, including a complete list of the duties and services the attorney is to perform. The agreement can be used as a checklist for gauging the performance of the attorney or agent.

The Attorney Retainer Agreement should document the manner in which you will pay the attorney or agent for legal services. This should include amounts, payment dates, and all other terms and conditions regarding payment of legal fees.

The Attorney Retainer Agreement provides that you can terminate your agreement at any time and for any reason. Your attorney or agent can also terminate the agreement for valid cause, such as your noncooperation or nonpayment, or with your consent. The agreement also provides for the immediate refund of the money paid to your attorney or agent if the agreement is terminated—except to deduct payment for time, costs, and expenses from your refund or credit.

The agreement obligates your attorney or agent to maintain your information in confidence and to give you or any new attorney or agent a copy of all documents in your file at your request. Any additional terms that you or your attorney or agent may have can be added to the agreement.

Both you and your attorney or agent should sign the agreement. Keep a copy of the fully signed agreement for your records.

## ATTORNEY RETAINER AGREEMENT

1. This is an Agreement made as of the_____day of_____, 19___, between (Client's name) _____ (Client's address) _____
(hereinafter referred to as the "Client") and
(Attorney's name)_____
(Attorney's address) _____
(hereinafter referred to as the "Attorney"), which defines the terms and conditions under which Client has retained Attorney to provide legal counsel and services relating to the following matter (describe the subject matter of the invention, patent, license or other legal issues of the Client):

_____
_____
_____

(hereinafter referred to as "Client's Case").

2. Attorney agrees to provide competent legal counsel and services to Client in connection with Client's Case and to perform the services provided below: (e.g., conduct prior art search, review patentability of invention, prepare U.S. patent application, prepare license agreement, handle patent litigation)

_____
_____

3. In consideration of the legal counsel and services performed by Attorney, Client agrees to make payment to Attorney as follows: (e.g., hourly rate, fixed fee, time period for payment)

_____
_____

4a. Client agrees to pay all reasonable costs and expenses incurred by Attorney in connection with Client's Case. Attorney estimates in good faith that these costs are as follows:

_____
_____

4b. Attorney agrees to obtain Client's prior approval before incurring any costs and any other expenses on behalf of Client in an amount greater than $_____.

5. Client has the right to terminate this Agreement at any time at Client's discretion. Attorney may terminate this agreement for valid cause upon Client's consent, provided that Client's Case is not prejudiced or harmed thereby.

6. Upon termination of this Agreement by either Client or Attorney, Client shall be entitled to the immediate refund or credit of all amounts paid or due, except as provided below:

_____

_____

7. After termination of this Agreement, Attorney agrees to provide to any new attorney or to Client, upon Client's request, a copy of all documents which Attorney has possession of relating to Client's Case.

8. Attorney shall maintain information regarding Client's Case in confidence and shall not disclose or use said information except for the benefit of Client as provided herein.

9. Additional terms and conditions:

Client and Attorney, intending to be legally bound, have signed this Agreement on the date first indicated above.

_____    _____
CLIENT'S SIGNATURE                                  ATTORNEY'S SIGNATURE

# CHAPTER 6

# Maintaining Confidentiality of Your Ideas

THERE ARE SEVERAL REASONS for maintaining the secrecy of an idea or invention and restricting or preventing its disclosure to others. You may want to keep your idea confidential to prevent someone else from stealing it before you can obtain legal protection for it. You may also want to maintain the confidentiality of your idea to retain your ability to file for a patent in the United States or foreign countries. Many countries require that there be no public use, sale, or disclosure of the invention before the date on which a patent application covering the invention is filed (the so-called absolute novelty requirement). Thus, initially maintaining confidentiality of your idea or invention allows you to protect it later for optimum commercial exploitation.

It is wise to maintain the confidentiality of your idea or invention until the patent has been granted because of the secret nature of a pending U.S. patent application (legislation to have the application published eighteen months after filing has been proposed). Do not publicly use or sell your invention while the patent application is pending before the PTO if it can be analyzed or reverse engineered to the point that it is no longer secret. During the pendency of the patent application, the invention or idea may be kept as a trade secret. Take adequate security measures to maintain the secrecy of the information to keep it a trade secret. If the patent application is not allowed by the PTO and is finally rejected, the application may go abandoned and, as long as it is not referred to in any other application that issues a U.S. patent, the idea or invention stays secret.

## Disclosing Your Ideas to Others in Confidence

To protect and exploit your ideas and inventions from a practical standpoint, you will need to disclose the nature of the ideas and inventions to outside parties, such as witnesses to the invention, model makers, employees, draftspeople, patent attorneys, invention promoters, consultants, and manufacturers. Otherwise, you will not be able to have the invention tested, patented, licensed, manufactured, or sold. Minimize disclosure of your ideas or inventions to those who have a need to know in order to help you protect or exploit your ideas or inventions. Disclose your ideas and inventions only after outside parties agree in writing to keep the information confidential.

When someone reviews the invention or a description of it and signs the invention documentation as a witness, he or she has an implied obligation to keep the details of the invention in confidence. Rather than rely on this implied confidentiality obligation, ask the witness to sign a written confidentiality agreement.

Likewise, your employees, agents, and consultants may be under an implied obligation of confidentiality, however, ask each of them to sign an appropriate written confidentiality agreement. Include provisions prohibiting your employees and consultants from stealing your ideas or inventions for the purpose of competing with you, and, furthermore, require them to assign to you any improvements they make on your inventions. These types of provisions are standard in most employment and consultant agreements.

When submitting your ideas to companies for their review and evaluation, state the purpose and advantages of your invention in one brief paragraph, and require the company to sign a confidentiality agreement before it obtains more detailed information. A sample confidentiality agreement is provided at the end of this chapter for use in situations where you will be disclosing your ideas or inventions to companies and others. Make sure that the person signing on behalf of the company is, or represents himself or herself to be, in a position to bind the company to the agreement. Language to that effect has been included in the sample confidentiality agreement.

Many companies may refuse to sign a confidentiality agreement before reviewing the idea. If such a company is important to getting your idea to market, you may have to disclose your idea even if it is unwilling to enter into a confidentiality agreement. If the idea is patented or otherwise protected, there is less risk in disclosing it. However, when you disclose unprotected ideas without a confidentiality agreement, mark the copies confidential and indicate in a letter to the company that the idea is submitted in confidence.

When you discuss your ideas and inventions with a patent attorney or patent agent, he or she is generally under a professional duty to maintain the confidentiality of your privileged information. If the attorney or agent violates this duty of confidentiality, he or she can face professional discipline and liability for damages caused to you by the unauthorized disclosure of your ideas. It is recommended that you enter into an Attorney Retainer Agreement that specifically obligates the patent attorney or agent to keep your ideas in confidence and not use or disclose them to others without your consent.

To protect the confidentiality of your ideas and to guard against theft when dealing with invention promoters and brokers, require them to sign a confidentiality agreement, as discussed earlier. If the broker steals your invention or idea, despite signing a confidentiality agreement, the broker may be "judgment proof". That is, the broker may have no assets from which you can extract monetary damages for the theft. Therefore, require the broker to provide you with evidence of professional liability insurance or bonding or both, before disclosing your ideas or inventions, so that you know the broker's compliance with the agreement is reasonably guaranteed.

## Handling Proprietary Information as a Business Owner

Whether you are a sole proprietor or a corporate business owner, the handling and transfer of confidential or proprietary information requires care and discretion. This is especially true when parties are dealing with intellectual property, such as invention disclosures, patent applications, and trade secrets, that can be extremely valuable to the success of a business.

Confidential trade secret information can include, without limitation, any formula, pattern, device, plan, process, or compilation of information that (1) is, or is designed to be, used in business, (2) is private or confidential in that it is not generally known or available to the public, and (3) gives the business an opportunity to obtain an advantage over competitors who do not know or use it. Take protective measures to maintain trade secrets, as discussed later in this chapter.

The research, technical, and marketing information of a business is usually confidential and proprietary information. Such information should not be disclosed outside of the business and should be kept confidential within the business (with certain exceptions). Employees of a business should not, without authority, either during the term of employment or thereafter (1) use or disclose any such confidential information outside the business, (2) publish any article with respect thereto, or (3) remove or aid in the removal from the premises of the business any such confidential information or any property or material which relates thereto.

Be concerned about safeguarding information that is critical to your business. The major factor to consider in assessing the criticality of information is what effect the loss or misuse might have on the competitive position, financial standing, employee relations, etc., of your business. This information can have varying degrees of criticality and you may want to classify this information accordingly.

For example, you may want to classify some information as "Strictly Confidential." This marking should be used to identify critically important information concerning technological breakthroughs, new product plans, acquisition plans, privileged financial data, etc. Information that is strictly confidential must be rigidly controlled while plans are being formulated, until the information or process is protected by other means (patents, license agreements, etc.), or the information has lost its critical degree of importance.

The test to determine if information is strictly confidential is whether this information, if published, could cause you considerable material damage to the point of endangering, in whole or in part, the very existence of the business. If the answer is yes, the information should be classified strictly confidential. Examples of documents that are strictly confidential include long-range strategic plans, critical chemical formulas, merger and acquisition plans, operational plans, important patent applications, and research and technical reports.

Mark or stamp "Strictly Confidential" on the cover, at least, of all documents containing such information. The information should not be made available to anyone but those persons on the distribution list. Such information should never be left unattended, and it should be kept under lock and key.

Documents marked strictly confidential should only be copied by the owner of the information. Copies should be numbered and should contain a distribution list and their issue and distribution should be monitored. The transmission of strictly confidential information via telefax or electronic mail should only be allowed when the information is encrypted or when it is ensured at both the sending and receiving end that only authorized personnel are operating the machines. Only pass on information that is strictly confidential to third parties when it is in the best interest of your business and subject to a written confidentiality agreement. Shred and destruct documents that are strictly confidential when they are no longer needed, and document the destruction of such documents.

Moderately important information, such as comparatively short-range plans, financial reports that are not extremely sensitive, impending announcements of significant personnel or organization changes, and manufacturing methods, should be considered confidential. Examples of other confidential documents include documents involving lawsuits, legal opinions, purchase contracts, trade agreements, certain customer correspondence, financial statements, budgets, forecasts, projections, and market share.

The word "Confidential" should be conspicuously marked on each document containing such information. Try not to overmark documents as confidential if they are not truly confidential. If, because of content or necessarily broad distribution of a particular document, it is unlikely that the document can receive the protection prescribed for documents marked confidential, it should not be classified as confidential.

Employees should have their proposed speeches and articles reviewed and approved by appropriate company personnel to make sure that confidential information is not being inadvertently disclosed. Make sure that employees leave company documents behind when they leave the company. Remind departing employees during their exit interviews of their duty to maintain the confidentiality of the company's proprietary information.

Any program to protect a company's confidential information must be tailored to the nature of the information and the needs of the particular company. Certainly, in any event, a company should identify its confidential information, establish reasonable programs to protect them, and conduct periodic checks to make sure the programs are working.

## Protecting the Confidentiality of Trade Secrets

Confidential trade secret information may embrace customer lists, technical data, commercial plans, sources of raw materials, and a variety of other proprietary information. Public disclosure of this type of information destroys the trade secret thereby permitting a competitor's use of it. Therefore, take affirmative steps to maintain the confidentiality of trade secrets.

The subject matter that qualifies for trade secret protection is broad. Almost any information or method used in business can be a trade secret if it is not generally known and proper precautions are taken to maintain its secrecy. Trade secrets can be applied to a formula, pattern, compilation, program, device, technique, or process. Thus, trade secrets may include chemical processes, key ingredients, process equipment, plant designs, raw material suppliers, customer lists, and other proprietary information. If reasonable and appropriate precautions are not taken to prevent disclosure of a trade secret to, or observation by, an outside party, then trade secret protection may be lost.

Courts have found the measures taken to protect trade secrets to be adequate where the owner of the trade secret took precautions to protect the confidential nature of its production process and equipment. These precautions were established by building a fence around the facility, limiting access to the facility, employing security guards to monitor premises, distributing confidential information only to employees who needed to know the information, and requiring all employees to sign employment agreements that obligated them to safeguard confidential information. The courts have also found adequate measure where the owner of the trade secret marked all information relating to the secret as confidential and used coded symbols to represent process ingredients and conditions.

On the other hand, trade secrets have not been protected when employees were given no indication as to what specific subject matter was confidential, when no signs were posted in areas where the trade secrets were located, where there were no locked fences or guard at the facility, when blueprints and drawings involving the trade secrets were left on the floor and in trash containers, when visitors were permitted to tour the facility without a confidentiality agreement, or when the trade secret was published in a magazine or the company's annual report.

## Security of Electronic Data

Treat electronic media containing confidential data with the same care and respect as confidential paper documents. Confidential data can reside on the file server, as well as on the workstation hard disk or on floppies. Take adequate security measures for this data. At a minimum, sensitive data that are kept locally should be locked (in a safe or equivalent, or in the case of the hard disk, by locking the computer with a power-on password) and backed up regularly with the backup kept secure. Store diskettes in locked containers.

Electronic mail systems (e-mail) provide easy access to many linked computers worldwide. It would be prudent to exercise some caution about assuming the confidentiality of e-mail messages.

Ultimately, individual users must assess the appropriateness of e-mail for sensitive messages. Consider the risk and the benefits of this method versus others. Generally, e-mail is more secure than sending documents to an unattended fax and it provides the confirmation of receipt. The security of e-mail depends, however, on the computer system being protected by passwords, and the intended user providing proper protection of the password.

## Using the Sample Confidentiality Agreement

A sample confidentiality agreement is provided at the end of this chapter. The sample confidentiality agreement is adaptable for use in practically any situation where proprietary information and ideas are disclosed to others.

The first paragraph of the sample confidentiality agreement identifies parties to the agreement, their addresses, and the effective date of the agreement. Paragraphs two and three identify the purpose of the agreement and describe the nature of the information to be disclosed and protected. Paragraph four recites the obligations of the recipient to maintain the confidentiality of the information and states that the recipient not use the disclosed information except as provided. It also provides that the recipient is not given any rights to the information that is disclosed. Additional paragraphs determine the return or destruction of the information that is disclosed or provided, and identify the state law that is to be applied in case of disputes and other terms.

The duration of confidentiality in a confidentiality agreement is typically a negotiated term dependent upon, among other things, the relative negotiating power of the parties and the relative importance of the confidential information. If one of the parties to the agreement is involved because of a special skill or indispensable expertise, that party can often influence the term of confidentiality in its favor. Also, if the confidential information represents a vitally important discovery or information that is fundamental to the success of a party, that party would likely require a relatively longer period of confidentiality. Typical time periods of confidentiality are three to ten years, although you should seek as long a period as possible (e.g., twenty years) when disclosing your confidential information.

Other terms and conditions may be added to the confidentiality agreement depending on the particular circumstances (e.g., broker situation). After full agreement on the terms and conditions, the agreement should be signed and dated by both the recipient and the discloser.

## CONFIDENTIALITY AGREEMENT

1. This Agreement is made on this_____day of_____, 19___ ("Effective Date") by and between _____(Discloser's name) _____(Discloser's address) and _____ (Recipient's name) _____(Recipient's address).

In consideration of the mutual covenants hereinafter set forth and other valuable consideration, the parties hereto agree to the following terms and conditions:

2. Discloser shall disclose to Recipient confidential and proprietary Information of Discloser relating to (describe subject matter to be disclosed):

3. Recipient shall use said Information of Discloser only for the purpose of (describe the reasons for Recipient to receive and review Discloser's Information):

4. Recipient shall maintain said Information of Discloser in confidence for a term of _____ years from disclosure hereof, and shall not disclose said Information to any party, and shall not use said Information in any way whatsoever, except as expressly provided herein. Nothing contained in this Agreement shall be deemed to give Recipient any rights whatsoever in and to said Information.

5. Upon the written request of Discloser, Recipient shall return all the Information of Discloser, or destroy such Information at the option of Discloser, except that one (1) copy of such Information may be retained by Recipient, solely for the purpose of monitoring its ongoing obligations hereunder.

6. The obligations of confidentiality and nonuse hereunder shall not apply to any Information which is or becomes publicly available through no fault of Recipient, or which was already known by Recipient before disclosure by Discloser as evidenced by written documents and records.

7. This Agreement shall be effective until _____ years after the Effective Date of this Agreement.

8. This Agreement shall be binding upon and shall inure to the benefit of the parties and their respective heirs, successors, assigns, and legal representatives.

9. This Agreement constitutes the entire agreement of the parties with respect to the subject matter hereof and shall not be amended orally, but only by an agreement in writing signed by both parties that states that it is an amendment to this Agreement.

10. This Agreement shall be governed by the laws of the State of _____.

11. Each person signing this Agreement as Discloser or Recipient hereby represents that he/she is authorized to sign on behalf of the party represented by him/her.

AGREED TO AND ACCEPTED BY:

_____          _____
DISCLOSER'S SIGNATURE                      RECIPIENT'S SIGNATURE


_____          _____
DATE                                       DATE

# Determining If Your Invention Is Patentable

KNOWING AS SOON AS POSSIBLE whether your invention is patentable is important if you will be spending significant amounts of time and money on patenting and commercializing it. Patentability depends on a number of factors, such as the type, utility, and novelty of the invention, as well as its unobviousness in view of the known prior art. You can always file a patent application on an invention and let the PTO review and determine whether it is patentable. It is preferable to search and review the relevant prior art before spending a lot of effort and resources on an unpatentable and otherwise unprotectable invention.

Unfortunately, not everyone who creates or develops something has a patentable invention within the laws and regulations of the PTO. There are a number of criteria that must be met and a number of traps and pitfalls that can render an otherwise patentable invention nonpatentable. Even though you may be able to evaluate the patentability of the invention yourself, it may be prudent to seek out the help of a patent attorney or agent.

## What Is a Patentable Invention?

Over the years, Congress, through legislation, and the courts, through case law in this area, have created rules and guidelines that provide a basis for determining which inventions are entitled to patent protection. An inventor must evaluate his or her invention against the required criteria, and if these criteria are met, there is a strong likelihood patent protection of some degree will be available.

Remember that before you can have a patentable invention, there must first be "conception" and "reduction to practice." Conception is the mental formulation of the invention in sufficient detail that someone familiar with the subject matter to which the invention relates could make and use the invention. Reduction to practice is generally making or constructing the invention (e.g., preparing a model or composition) and testing it to demonstrate its usefulness for its conceived purpose.

Your invention must fall within the required statutory classes for patentable invention to qualify for a U.S. utility patent. These classes include processes, machines, articles of manufacture, compositions of matter, or any improvements thereon. Statutory classes will be discussed in greater detail later.

In order for an invention to be patentable in the United States, it must be new or novel, useful, and unobvious.

Basically, for an invention to be new or novel, as required by the U.S. patent laws, the invention must not have been previously known by others. For example, you cannot obtain a patent if (1) your invention has been described in a printed publication anywhere in the world, or it has been in public use or on sale in the United States before the date you made your invention, or (2) your invention has been described in a printed publication anywhere or been in public use or on sale for more than one year before you filed your patent application.

A patent cannot be obtained even though the invention is new if the difference between the subject matter sought to be patented and the prior art are such that the subject matter "as a whole" would have been "obvious," at the time the invention was made, to a person having "ordinary skill in the art" to which the subject matter pertains. The determination of obviousness of an invention is a legal issue based on rules from court decisions.

For an invention to be unobvious, the invention need not have been the result of some flash of genius, nor require a synergistic result. If an invention merely utilizes the teachings or suggestions of the prior art to solve a problem and no unexpected results are obtained, it is doubtful that the invention overcomes the obviousness test. The invention must be evaluated on the basis of how it relates to the problem faced, the need for a solution, how it differs from the prior art, what features are not taught or suggested from the prior art, and its prospects of commercial success.

The usefulness requirement can be easily met by showing any kind of utility for the invention. Where a special utility is being claimed for the invention (e.g., a cure for cancer), it will have to be demonstrated by appropriate testing.

## The Statutory Classes of Patentable Inventions

The U.S. patent laws provide that in order for a utility invention to be patentable, it must fall within one of five classes:
- compositions of matter
- processes or procedures
- articles of manufacture
- machine
- a new and useful improvement on any of the above

A single patent may include more than one type of invention as long as each type is properly related to the other. These classes of patentable subject matter need not be specifically referred to in a patent, although the invention must fit into one or more of these classes.

### Composition of matter

A compound that refers to a new chemical entity, and the invention resides in the absolute novelty of the compound is a composition of matter. Compound inventions are rare in certain research areas, while in other areas, such as pharmaceutical and agricultural chemicals, many are the result of the discovery of a new compound having a medicinal or agricultural use. The new compound is not patentable solely because it is novel unless a use (utility) can be established.

A chemical composition refers to a combination of two or more compounds (i.e. a mixture). The invention resides in the use and combination of the composition. The combination must provide some new use or an improvement over the use of the individual components of the composition for the same use, if any component present in the composition is known to be useful for that use.

Anyone, other than the patentee, who makes, uses, or sells a patented composition without the patentee's permission will infringe the composition of matter claim. Composition of matter claims, therefore, can provide strong patent protection. To obtain patent protection for composition of matter, a compound or composition must be thoroughly analyzed and described in terms of its chemical structure (as in the case of a new compound), and/or its physical and chemical properties, or by its method of preparation. If the compound or composition is prepared by only one technique, claims to the product according to the process of its preparation may be included in the patent. The patent protection for a compound or composition that can only be defined by the process of its preparation (product-by-process) is generally not considered as strong as protection for composition of matter per se.

### Process

A process or method invention is the operation or series of steps that leads to a useful result. The synthesis of a new compound or composition or a new method for making a known product may be a patentable process invention. Process inventions may be made by those who discover the need for a new step or the need to select certain process parameters for some improved result, such as a better product or a higher yield.

A process that uses a computer program or mathematical formula to produce a physical result, such as the computer control of a process for producing a product, may be patentable. The mathematical formula or method of calculation is not patentable.

A use invention is closely related to a process invention and is commonly referred to as a process or method of use. The new use of an old product or process may be patentable.

### Article of Manufacture

Any item that does not fulfill the composition of matter, compound, process, or device categories will likely fall in the category of an article of manufacture. Articles of manufacture include nearly every man-made object from a paper clip to a skyscraper.

### Machine

Any mechanical or electrical apparatus or device is considered a machine, including a camera, a bicycle, a computer, or an airplane, or the like.

### Improvements

Any new, useful, and unobvious improvement on a composition of matter, process, article of manufacture, or machine can be protected by a patent. For example, the discovery of a new use for any of the first four statutory classes is also patentable, such as the use of a drug that is administered to cure one disease is discovered to be beneficial in the treatment of an entirely different disease or condition. Changes to a known composition, machine, article of manufacture, or process to achieve a better or different result may be patentable inventions. Even improvements on already patented inventions can be patentable.

## Utility

As mentioned earlier, one requirement that must be met for an invention to be patentable, as dictated by 35 United States Code (U.S.C.) Section 101 is that the invention be useful, otherwise known as having utility. Generally, any known utility will suffice, and the only caveat to keep in mind is that the utility must be functional and not merely aesthetic. Rather, aesthetic features are more suitable for design patent or copyright protection as discussed in chapter 2. Although nearly any invention can have utility or "usefulness" in one way or another, some otherwise inventive ideas could be denied patent protection by falling in one of the "not useful as a matter of law" statutory classes. These include illegal inventions and products, unproved and unsafe new drugs, whimsical inventions, immoral inventions, nonoperable inventions, and the like.

There must be some good derived from the use of the invention in order for it to be patentable. The good so derived need not be of any great degree or extent but need merely confer a benefit to the user in a defined manner. Thus, inventions that are considered destructive by their nature can still be useful and patentable such as a gun, explosive, nerve gas, or electric chair. If the invention provides any benefit to society, no matter how small or unusual, it will likely pass the utility test for obtaining a U.S. patent.

In many cases, a mere allegation of utility and operability by the inventor in a patent application is sufficient to meet the test, particularly if the allegation is apparent from the description of the invention. Utility and operability may have to be demonstrated in some cases where they are not apparant from a review of the invention such as cancer treatments, cures for baldness, and perpetual motion machines.

## Novelty and Anticipation

One requirement for patentability of an invention in the United States is that the invention be new or novel and not merely a copy or repetition of those of the past. The specific statutory requirements for novelty are provided by the patent laws in 35 United States Code Section 102, which is included in the Appendix.

To qualify as new under U.S. law an invention must:

1. not have been known, published, or used publicly anywhere by others before the invention was made by the patent applicant, or
2. not have been patented or described by anyone in a printed publication anywhere, or on sale in the United States more than one year prior to the date of filing the U.S. patent application, or
3. not have been abandoned by the patent applicant, or
4. not have been first patented in a foreign country prior to the date of the patent application based on an application filed more than twelve months before the filing of the U.S. application, or
5. not have been described in a patent granted to another where

the other patent application was filed in the United States before the invention by the patent applicant, or

6. not have been made in the United States by another before the invention by the patent applicant.

The failure of the invention to meet any one of the above criteria means the invention is not novel but was anticipated by the prior art and bars the right to a U.S. patent.

One issue that arises with respect to the effect of prior art, on what is and what is not patentable, is a concept known as anticipation. This bar to patentability is essentially the situation where each and every element of the invention can be found disclosed or described in a single prior art reference or source. For example, if you as an inventor combine elements $A + B + C + D$ to yield E, and there is a patent, scientific journal, or other publication that by itself teaches $A + B + C + D$ yields E, your invention is anticipated and will not be patentable.

In order for a single prior art reference to anticipate your invention, however, all the elements must be arranged in substantially the same way to achieve the same result as your invention. If for example, the prior art reference teaches that the elements must be arranged $B + D + C + A$ to yield E, your invention of $A + B + C + D$ yields E will not likely be anticipated and patent protection for your invention may be available. Further, if all of your elements are not described (e.g., the patent or article teaches that $A + B + C$ yields E), again there is no anticipation because each and every element of your invention must be found within the teachings of that reference, and here D is lacking.

A prior art reference may still anticipate your invention if one or more of the elements of your invention are inherently disclosed within that reference. In other words, an anticipatory reference need not duplicate word for word the elements of a claimed invention, but it is enough if some of the elements of the invention are inherent or otherwise implicitly described in that reference. For example, this time you've discovered that E possesses some feature or characteristic never before described or realized in the prior art. If a prior art reference discloses E without specifically describing that feature or property of E, your invention may still be anticipated by the reference if that feature is an inherent property of E. E possesses that property or characteristic regardless of whether or not that property was described in the reference.

Even if there is no existing prior art that may render your invention obvious or anticipated, you as the inventor can unfortunately take actions, which, by themselves, can defeat your right to a patent. These bars to patentability involve the premature disclosure, sale, or foreign patenting of your invention more than one year prior to filing a patent application in the United States or some other country covered by the Patent Cooperation Treaty (PCT).

The disclosure or sale of your invention, which will result in a bar to patentability, can happen in a number of ways. This may consist of the sale or mere offer of sale of the invention to others, advertising the invention or any other written publication thereof, audio and video disclosure of the invention, and any disclosure of the invention in a speech, journal article, or promotional literature. Any of these acts by you or by others whereby your invention is disclosed to the public more than one year before filing an appropriate patent application constitutes a bar to a U.S. patent for that invention.

Most foreign countries are not as compassionate toward inventors as the United States. Whereas the U.S. patent laws grant a one-year grace period for filing an application from the date of sale or publication, most foreign countries regard such acts of disclosure as absolute bars to patentability. That is, any act of a public disclosure of the invention prior to the filing of a patent application is an immediate bar to any patent rights in most countries. In such a case, there is no grace period in most of the world, including Europe, the Pacific Rim, and South America, and your rights to a patent on the invention in these countries will be forever lost.

There is the judicially created doctrine known as experimental use that makes an exception to the public use and disclosure bar. Although narrowly construed, certain inventions need to be tested by the inventor in order to determine whether they are workable. An example of experimental use is an old court case to decide whether the inventors discovered an improved asphalt for making roads. At the time, the only way the inventors could test whether or not the asphalt lasted longer, with less wear and tear, was to use it in a roadway. Although patentability was initially denied, the U.S. Supreme Court later concluded that, since public use was the only way the invention could be tested, disclosure of the composition through its incorporation in a public road was not a bar under the patent laws.

## Obviousness

The obviousness test is usually the toughest requirement to pass in obtaining a U.S. patent on your invention. Even if the invention is new and useful, it is not patentable unless there is some unobvious and unexpected result.

The obviousness test in practical effect prevents an inventor from getting a patent when all the elements of the invention are not found within a single prior art reference, but all the elements can be found when two or more references are combined. Again, you have invented A + B + C + D → E. One reference teaches the elements A + B. Another reference teaches the elements C + D. Your invention would likely be considered obvious because of these references if there is a basis for combining the references.

It is important for the obviousness test that the prior art references must in fact be combinative in order to lead one skilled in the art to the invention at issue. In essence, the references must in one way or another be related or at least concerned with the same field of endeavor to suggest to one skilled in the art the benefits of the combination. The PTO, once knowing your invention, cannot use hindsight and review the plethora of prior art references and selectively pick and choose the elements of your invention from various isolated and unrelated references that deal with different fields of study or inventive purpose.

For example, you've combined A + B + C + D to obtain E, which is a low-calorie fat replacer compound for use in foods. Suppose elements A and B are known thickeners in food products. And suppose element C is disclosed in reference #1 as an emulsifier in paints, while D is disclosed in reference #2 as a component in shampoos. Here one skilled in the art (e.g., a food scientist) would not be motivated to take something used in making paints and combine it with something used in shampoos to produce a food product. These references are not combinative to show obviousness because they do not suggest the use of elements C and D in anything even remotely similar to an edible food product. A similar situation exists where the prior art reference specifically teaches that one of the elements, C or D, cannot be used in food due to its bad taste or smell. This would not motivate one to combine it as an ingredient so as to come up with your invention.

Obviousness is a fairly gray area and not as cut-and-dry as the anticipation bar to patentability. Anticipation under 35 United States Code Section 102 is fairly black and white. Either all the elements of your invention are specifically or inherently disclosed within the four corners of a prior art reference or they are not. Obviousness, on the other hand, often depends on whether combining the references involved would be logical and reasonable, and even if so, whether all the elements of the invention are taught or suggested in the manner and for the purpose of the invention.

Many times, references used in rejecting an invention for obviousness teach more than the elements of the invention itself and may suggest that the elements can be used for other unrelated purposes. Whether partially unrelated references can be combined is always debatable, and even if the references are combinative, whether your invention would be the logical end result of the combination would also be an issue.

You must show that your invention provides surprising and unexpected results to prove that it is an invention and not obvious. You can do this by conducting comparative tests between your invention and the prior art to demonstrate the unexpected advantage of your invention.

Fortunately for inventors, the courts have interpreted the patent laws to allow other intangible aspects of inventions to be considered in determining patentability. Known as "secondary considerations" of nonobviousness, these aspects are factual or evidentiary features of the invention that may be used to show the invention is novel, useful, and nonobvious. Taken together, these secondary considerations are not all controlling or dispositive of the issue, but they will go a long way in proving the invention is worthy of patent protection.

The secondary considerations are:

- proof that the invention cures a need or solves a problem where others have often tried yet failed
- proof that the invention solves a problem that always existed but was never before recognized or, if recognized, thought to be unsolvable
- proof that the invention satisfies a long felt, unfulfilled need
- proof that the invention has already attained commercial success on its own merit
- proof that the invention achieves a desired purpose or result in a manner contrary to the beliefs or teachings of the prior art

## Maximizing the Patentability of Your Invention

Before creating your invention, define the problem with which you are faced or the objective you are trying to reach and record this information and these ideas. Review prior art to help generate potential solutions and to determine what ideas or inventions are new and patentable. These are some of the steps you should take to keep from reinventing the wheel and to enhance your chances of creating a patentable invention.

The following checklist will assist you in maximizing the likelihood of patent protection for your invention.

### Define the Problem or Objective

- Describe the technical area related the to problem or objective, or describe areas that are closely related.
- Describe the problem in detail, as well as the possible cause of the problem or the objective, including the economic and technical concerns. Alternately, describe the parameters and analytical techniques that may determine whether or not you have met your objective or solved the problem. Outline the steps you will have to take to ensure success.
- Describe all conventional products or processes known that have been tried to solve the problem or meet your objective, list their technical and economic successes or failures and limitations, and explain how your proposed idea differs from each of the prior techniques.

### Conduct a Literature Search

- Conduct a literature search and compile publications related to the problem, its cause, or your proposed solution, prior to conducting any experimental work. The literature search will inform you as to what others have proposed as solutions and may help you avoid wasting time on rediscovering known inventions.

- Frame a search request and strategy for conducting a literature search to find all published articles, patents, and published patent applications relating to your problem and your possible solution. Make a list of keywords that generally define the problem and your conception of its solution. Precise definitions of the best keywords will be important in conducting effective literature searches. A patent attorney or patent searcher can assist in uncovering patents in the areas related to your problem. Patent searchers or information retrieval specialists are usually trained to conduct searches not only of published patents, but also of journal articles and other documents published worldwide. They use a variety of computer data-bases such as Derwent, Chemical Abstracts, and Lexis.

- Review the search results carefully and obtain copies of all the relevant publications and patents. Digest all the references and analyze which approaches have been taken in the past, as well as which approaches have not been taken and why. This information will help you determine whether you should proceed to make your invention and will maximize your chances of getting a patent.

- Formulate a research strategy to make your invention after your initial analysis of the literature search is complete. Write a concise statement of your idea when you get an idea of how to solve your problem. This statement should include all the parameters you believe are necessary for solving the problem and as many individual features, elements, compounds, compositions, or processes that might be necessary for your idea to work. Then, describe how you plan to proceed to prove whether your idea actually is the answer to solving the problems you defined earlier.

- Explore all the variables of your invention—this includes

materials of construction, ranges for each component in a composition, substituents on a structure, molecular weights, temperatures, pressures, etc. Also explore the outer limits of your invention to obtain the broadest patent coverage needed for the invention. An invention is not completely defined until you know how to change each of the variables to determine when the invention works and when it does not. This type of experimentation is the only true way to define the scope of the invention, the preferred embodiment(s) of the invention, and the best products or methods to practice your invention.

- Describe your invention fully after testing the limits of it in a systematic way. This description will help you and your attorney or agent to draft a patent application covering everything that works (and is not disclosed or suggested in prior publications), while eliminating those that do not work. An overly broad patent that claims items which do not work is to be avoided just as an unduly narrow patent, because overly broad patent claims can be challenged as invalid. By employing this systematic approach to testing, you will not leave holes in the patent protection or provide avenues for others to avoid your patent by working around the invention you have defined.

# CHAPTER 8

# Preparing and Filing a U.S. Patent Application

AFTER REVIEWING THE PRIOR ART and determining that your invention is patentable and economically viable, you should file for patent protection on the invention. If you are a U.S. inventor, the easiest process is to file a regular or provisional patent application with the PTO. You can begin this process by hiring a good patent attorney or agent, or you can prepare and file the patent application yourself if you have a good understanding of how to draft a sufficient patent application and get it filed at the PTO.

This chapter provides step-by-step instructions on how to prepare and file a simple U.S. patent application. These instructions will take you through the preparatory steps to writing the specification and claims, preparation of drawings, and completion of all other formalities. By following the process outlined in this chapter, you will be able to prepare a patent application that should successfully withstand the scrutiny of the PTO, licensees and assignees, and the federal courts. Approach the task with confidence and optimism that comes from being a patent-knowledgeable inventor and the best

person to describe your invention, and you will have little or no difficulty handling the preparation and filing of your patent application.

## Understanding the Format of a U.S. Patent Application

A complete U.S. patent application has several components, some
of which are mandatory and others that are optional. The mandatory
components of a U.S. patent application include (1) a specification
with one or more claims, (2) drawings, if necessary to describe or
disclose the invention, (3) the names of the inventors; (4) the
required declaration of inventorship, and (5) the requisite filing fee.

The specification, claims, and drawings in a patent application
become a part of the granted and published patent and normally
follow a specific format. The specification should consist of the
following parts:

1. title
2. reference to any related applications, if any
3. background of the invention
4. summary of the invention
5. brief description of the drawings, if any
6. detailed description of the invention
7. one or more claims
8. abstract

A specification with claims, necessary drawings, and names of
all inventors must be included in the patent application for it to be
given a filing date. A declaration and filing fee are also mandatory
for an application to be complete, but these can be submitted within
two months of filing the application without losing the original filing
date.

In addition to the above mandatory items, the following optional
items should also accompany a completed application: an Application Transmittal Letter, an Information Disclosure Statement, a
Verified Statement of Small Entity Status (if applicable), an Assignment (if applicable), and a self-addressed return postcard to
acknowledge receipt of the application by the PTO.

The specification is the core of a completed patent application.
Before you begin drafting the specification, it is a good idea to do

the following preliminary work to prepare to write the specification:

1. Become familiar with the patent regulations. There are three sets of statutes or regulations that govern all patent matters. The first two are the Patent Statute, 35 United States Code (U.S.C.), and the Patent Rules, 37 Code of Federal Regulations (C.F.R.), a more detailed set of regulations based on the Patent Statute. All the requirements for drafting an application can be found in the Patent Statute and the Patent Rules. Copies are available from the GPO and can be ordered by telephone (202/ 512-1800). Also, if you have access to the Internet you can visit the GPO at *http://www.access.gpo.gov*

   The third set of rules governing patent procurement is the Manual of Patent Examiner's Procedures (MPEP), which is followed by the patent examiners in reviewing applications. You probably do not need this 1,500-page manual to draft a patent application, but it could be useful in prosecuting the application. The Patent and Trademark Depository Libraries listed in the Appendix should have a copy. The MPEP is also available from the GPO as well as through the Internet site of the PTO at *http://www.uspto.gov/*

2. Write a brief (one to three paragraphs) description of the invention. Include all the unique elements and variations of the invention in this description.

3. List the advantages and benefits of the invention, particularly those that are surprising and unexpected.

4. If the invention requires drawings to fully describe or disclose it, make preliminary sketches and number all relevant parts in the drawings. Use as many views as necessary to fully describe and disclose the invention. These sketches are important as they are the basis for the formal drawings that will become part of the application and granted patent.

5. Review all relevant prior art you that you have located. You can use this art to generate terminology to describe your invention and to see how similar inventions are described and drawn. Refer to this prior art in the background section of the specification. Finally, submit copies of the prior art to the PTO with an Information Disclosure Statement. The Information Disclosure Statement will be discussed later.

6. Draft a sample claim, one sentence, to describe the invention and the necessary elements of the invention. A claim is a formalized, precise description of the invention. For further explanation, see the discussion on drafting claims later in this chapter.
7. Review other U.S. patents in the field of your invention to help you decide how to organize your application. Since U.S. patents are not protected by copyright law, sections of text from these patents can be copied and included in your application.

After you have completed these preliminary steps, you should have a good understanding of what your invention is and what unique elements you will be able to claim. When you are satisfied that you know your invention, and you can describe it in words and drawings, you are ready to begin drafting the specification.

## Drafting the Patent Specification

The specification, along with the drawings and claims, is published in the granted patent. At the end of the specification are one or more claims that specifically defines the invention and all the required elements. Because the claims are such a unique and important part of the specification, they are discussed in greater detail later in this chapter. The specification is a detailed description of the invention that must fully disclose everything one needs to know, as well as the inventor's best mode, to practice the invention.

The full disclosure requirement for patent applications is mandated by 37 Code of Federal Regulations, Section 112, first paragraph, of the Patent Statute, which states:

> The specification shall contain a written description of the invention, and of the manner and process of making and using it, in such full, clear, concise and exact terms as to enable any person skilled in the art to which it pertains, or with which it is most nearly connected, to make and use the same, and shall set forth the best mode contemplated by the inventor of carrying out his invention.

It is critically important that your patent specification meet the requirements of the first paragraph of Section 112. These requirements basically mean that (1) the specification must adequately describe the invention, (2) the specification must teach or enable someone else who has skill in the technical area of the invention to make and use the invention, and (3) the specification must present the best way known by the inventor for practicing the invention.

There are a number of reasons why it is imperative that your application meet the requirements of the patent statute when you file the application. First, failure to meet these requirements can result in a rejection of your application by the PTO or in a subsequent finding of patent invalidity should the granted patent ever be litigated. Second, after the patent application has been filed, you are not allowed to add new information (called "new matter") without refiling the application. Third, everything you claim as your invention must be in the specification.

Other requirements for the specification are that it be typed on either letter- (8½" × 11"), legal- (8½" × 13" or 14"), or A4-size (21 × 29.7 cm) paper. Spacing between lines should be set at 1.5 or double space. The specification, claims, and abstract should each begin on a new page. Use the following margins for letter and legal-sized paper: at least 1½" at the top and bottom, and at least 1" on the right and left. Number each page of the specification, preferably at the bottom.

Many foreign patent offices require that the application be filed on A4-size paper. The margin requirements for this size of paper are slightly different: top, left, and right margins must be at least 2 cm; the bottom margin must be at least 2.5 cm. If you are planning to also file your application outside the United States, it may be easier if you use A4-size paper and margins requirements for both applications.

Let's review the parts of the specification.

## 1. Title

Sometimes the most difficult part of drafting a patent application is putting the first words on paper or into your word processor. Put a title at the top of the first page to help you get started. The title should be descriptive and state, in just a few words, the essence of your invention. It is acceptable to use laudatory words in the title such as "An Improved Cleaning Solution" or "A Novel Can Opener." Remember that the title is a required item of the application, thus writing it down will help get you one step closer to completing the application.

### 2. References to related applications

If you have previously filed any applications for the same or one or more related inventions, reference those applications at the beginning of the patent specification. For example, you should use language such as, "This application is a [continuation/continuation-in-part/divisional] of application Serial No._____, filed on_____, entitled '_____.'"

Omit this item if there are no related applications.

### 3. Background of the invention

This item of the specification provides information about the field of the invention and describes the current state of the art. Discuss the prior art and how your invention is distinguishable from it. Explain the objectives and advantages of your invention. For example, you can make a statement such as, "One objective of this invention is to provide a can opener that can be operated with one hand. A further objective of this invention is to provide a collapsible can opener that can be operated with one hand." Stating the objectives in this manner is a way to try to persuade a patent examiner that your invention is unique and patentable.

### 4. Summary of the invention

Include a brief synopsis of the invention and its benefits. Begin by summarizing the objectives identified earlier. Then the subject matter of the invention should be described in one or more clear, concise sentences or paragraphs. In many cases, the summary of the invention can simply be a recitation of the main claim in the application and a brief explanation of the elements of the invention.

### 5. Brief description of the drawings

If the application includes drawings, provide a brief description of them in the specification. This part of the application typically begins with a sentence such as, "The accompanying drawings further describe the invention." After that introduction, in separate paragraphs, write only one or two sentences describing the drawings such as, "Figure 1 is a perspective view of the gear shift constructed in accordance with the invention."

### 6. Detailed description of the invention

The detailed description is the most comprehensive item in the specification. In this section of the specification, describe the invention fully, clearly, concisely, and exactly to enable a technically skilled person to make and use the invention without extensive experimentation. Disclose the best mode known by you for practicing the invention, and disclose every element of your invention that you plan to claim.

Prepare an outline of the detailed description of the invention before you begin to write it. Make certain you have sketched all the drawings you plan to use and have labeled and numbered all elements. Name and describe each numbered element in the detailed description.

In a typical patent application, the few paragraphs of the detailed description introduces the invention by describing it in broad terms. With this broad description as a beginning, you can then describe the invention in greater and greater detail. The beginning of the detailed description should be like the base of a pyramid or the trunk of a tree from which the rest of the description will emerge.

As you write the specification, name all elements of the invention that you plan to claim. Finding the appropriate name for an element is important and can be tricky. Here are a few suggestions to help in defining elements of your invention. Keep in mind that a patent applicant can be a lexicographer. In other words, you define the elements and terms of your invention. For example, if the invention is a novel antiseptic composition, you could state, "In this invention, antiseptic means a composition that kills microorganisms or prevents or inhibits their growth and reproduction." Use a thesaurus, dictionary, or glossary of technical terms for assistance. Avoid using nonspecific terms such as "gadget," "thing," or "widget." After you have selected a name for an element, use that name consistently throughout the specification and do not use different names interchangeably.

After describing the invention in broad terms and defining all its important elements, describe each element of the invention as specifically as possible. For example, if the invention is a one-handed, collapsible can opener that includes the elements of a handle and a cutting edge, describe for each element the shape, size, and materials that it could be made of, and any other relevant characteristics. If the invention is a new composition, the elements are the ingredients in the composition. Identify every ingredient and all possible examples of each ingredient. If the invention is a process, the elements are the steps of the process such as mixing, heating, or drying. Describe each step in complete detail, stating mixing time, heating temperature, and drying conditions. Err on the side of being overly inclusive, since new matter cannot be added to the application once it has been filed.

Make sure you identified and described, in detail, each element of the invention. Keep the requirements of 35 United States Code Section 112, first paragraph, in mind (e.g., fully disclose, enable, and teach the best mode). This portion of the application might include several pages if the invention has many elements, ingredients, or steps. On the other hand, if there are only one or two elements in the invention, this description will be much shorter. Whether it is long or short, however, the description must completely describe and disclose the invention.

Identify the "preferred" and "most preferred" embodiments of the invention in the detailed description. If a component can be made of several different materials, identify these by stating, "Preferred materials for the handle of the can opener of this invention are aluminum, tin, and stainless steel." You can then narrow the description even more by stating, "The most preferred material for the handle is stainless steel." You will then have a basis in the claims for drafting increasingly more specific or narrower claims directed to the preferred and most preferred materials.

Because specificity is critical in an application, the use of trade-marks instead of generic names for components or ingredients should be avoided, unless the mark is necessary for full identi-fication. Use generic names when possible; for example, instead of

Velcro®, use "hook and loop fastener," instead of Scotch Tape®, say "plastic tape."

It is optional whether to include any examples of making, using, or testing the invention in the detailed description. Examples are not required in a U.S. patent application, but they can be useful in describing the invention and demonstrating patentability to the examiner. In a U.S. patent application, you can even use prophetic or hypothetical examples (provided you show them as such, for example, "The invention could be made by . . ." or "If the invention were made by . . ."). But actual examples may be needed for filing in some foreign countries with stricter requirements. If you have created one or more working models of the invention, you should describe them in the detailed description under a subpart entitled Examples. If you have experimented with the invention, you should include the experimental results in the examples.

If the invention includes drawings, correlate the elements in the drawings and their description in the specification. When you refer to an element of the invention in the specification, you should name it and refer to it by its drawing number (for example, "the handle 12" or "a hinge 13"). Refer to the elements in the drawings in numerical order. You could start by assigning only even reference numbers (e.g., 2, 4, . . .) to the elements. That way, as you complete the description you can add new elements and reference numbers without upsetting the numerical order of the description.

Your U.S. patent application must include the best mode contemplated by you or any coinventors for practicing the invention. Thus, you cannot keep important parts of your invention secret and obtain a U.S. patent on it. You can describe the best mode for carrying out the invention in the detailed description or include it in the examples. Because you do not have to refer to the best mode as such, or otherwise highlight it, you can effectively bury it within the patent application.

Every element or feature included in the patent claims must find support in the patent specification. Again, identify and describe every critical and claimed feature of your invention in the detailed description. Copy the wording of the claims into the detailed description to make certain that all elements in the claims have an antecedent basis in the description.

Briefly summarize the invention and its benefits and advantages at the end of the detailed description. There is a good deal of repetition in a patent application, but this repetition can help you sell the invention and its patentability.

You want your patent application to be interpreted as broadly as legally possible and do not want to restrict the scope of the invention unless absolutely necessary. To help ensure a broad interpretation, a short statement such as the following is useful:

The above description and examples should be not construed as limitations on the scope of the invention. Many other variations are possible. Accordingly, the scope of the invention is determined by the claims and their legal equivalents.

### 7. Abstract

The abstract is presented on a separate sheet of paper at the end of the specification after the claims. When the patent is published the abstract will appear on the first page. The abstract should be no more than a 250-word summary of the invention. The purpose of the abstract is to disclose the novel elements of the invention and to help the examiner and the public quickly determine the nature of the technical disclosure. Writing the abstract should be relatively simple after you have completed the rest of the specification, and, for simplicity, it could be a summary of the main patent claim.

### 8. Title page

Remember that one requirement of a completed application is to include names of the inventors and a title page meets this requirement. The title page includes the title of the invention, the names of the inventors, and, if possible, the addresses of each inventor. Identify all inventors of the invention on your title page. Failure to include the correct inventor(s) could result in a patent being held unenforceable. If there is more than one inventor, the order of their names is legally irrelevant, except that the name of first-named inventor will be used to identify the patent.

## The Claims

The claims are the last part of the specification and are perhaps the most important part of the patent application. Claims are numbered sentences that define the patentable invention. The patent statute provides that the specification shall conclude with one or more claims particularly pointing out and distinctly claiming the subject matter which the applicant regards as his or her invention.

The claims must describe the invention clearly enough so that anyone reading them knows the scope, or the "metes and bounds," of the invention.

It is a good technique to draft the claims from an outline of the important elements of the invention—even before you start to write the detailed description. Drafting patent claims takes practice, and you may spend a good deal of time completing this portion of the patent application. You may want a skilled patent agent or attorney to review the claims and the rest of the application before you file to make sure the application is formatted correctly. The examiner in the PTO can help you draft allowable claims after you have filed an application with at least one claim.

Keep in mind Sections 102, 103, and 112, paragraphs two through six of the Patent Statute when drafting claims of your invention. Under Section 102, a patent will be granted only if the claimed invention is novel. Thus, recite the novel features of your invention in the claims. Claims to inventions that are not novel, under Section 102, are rejected by the PTO on the grounds of "anticipation" by the prior art. Under Section 103, claims in a patent application will be rejected if the PTO finds that the claimed invention is "obvious" in view of the prior art. The claims should be as broad as possible, yet narrow enough so the claimed invention is both novel and non-obvious. Good claim drafting requires balancing these conflicting considerations.

In addition, 35 United States Code Section 121 provides that each application must be for one "independent and distinct" invention. In other words, you cannot claim two unrelated inventions in the same application. The meaning of independent and distinct, however, is murky. Should you be uncertain whether you are claiming more than one invention, err on the side of being overly broad or inclusive. The PTO may require that you restrict the application to one invention, and you can make an election then.

As you may have observed from reading granted patents, the form and language of claims are highly stylized. The claims section begins with the statement, "What is claimed is . . .". Each claim is one, and only one, sentence. Each sentence, in turn has three components: a preamble, a transition, and a body. Let's review each component and the format of a patent claim.

### 1. Preamble of the claim

The preamble is a brief introductory statement that summarizes, describes, or defines the basic nature or class of the invention and precedes the body of the claim. The preamble can be general or specific depending on the character of the invention and the prior art. Typical preambles to claims are, "A composition . . . ," or "A composition for preventing oral malodor . . . ," or "An apparatus . . . ," or "An apparatus for opening metal containers . . ."

Usually, the preamble of a claim is given little or no weight in determining patentability of the claim. For this reason, it is important that all the critical elements of the invention be included in the body of the claim and not in the preamble.

### 2. Transitional phrase

Following the preamble is a transitional word or phrase connecting the preamble to the body of the claim. The broadest transitional words are "comprising" or "which comprises." These are called open transitional words. A claim with "comprising" or "which comprises" as a transition encompasses additional elements that are not specifically recited in the claim. For example, if what is claimed is, "A composition comprising A, B, and C," then one who makes a composition with A, B, C, and D would still be infringing the claim. In other words, any other composition with A, B, and C in it, even if it contained numerous other ingredients, would be an infringing composition. Therefore, it is preferable to use open transitional words to obtain the broadest possible patent coverage.

The narrowest transitional words are "consisting" or "consisting of." These are called closed transitional words. These words limit the claim only to those elements specifically recited in the claim. For example, if what is claimed is, "A composition consisting of A, B, and C," then the only infringing compositions would be those with only components A, B, and C; no more and no less. Use these closed transitional words only if the claims must be narrowed to overcome the prior art.

Between open and closed transitional words are partially closed transitional words, the best example of which is "consisting essentially of." In general, partially closed transitional words are used to overcome the prior art, yet they allow the claimed invention to encompass certain unrecited elements, provided these elements are not essential to define the novel and nonobvious aspects of the claimed invention. For example, if what is claimed is "A composition consisting essentially of A, B, and C," a composition made of A, B, C, and D, wherein D is not an essential component of the composition (e.g., it merely changes the color), would still infringe this claim.

### 3. Body of the claim

The body of the claim consists of (1) a statement of the elements of the invention and (2) a description of how these elements related to each other to make the invention. The elements of the invention are either the structural components of an article of manufacture or a machine, the ingredients of a composition of matter, or the steps of a process. These are the elements you include in the detailed description of the invention.

The fundamental principle of drafting claims is to include all the critical elements, regardless of the class of the invention. For example, if the invention is a machine for sorting bottles, the elements would consist of the parts of the machine. Similarly, if the invention is a new method for manufacturing plastic, the elements would include the steps of the new method or process. If the invention is a new laundry detergent, the elements would consist of the ingredients that comprise the detergent. Make sure the names of the elements in the claims are consistent throughout the specification.

The first time a new element is named in the claims it is preceded by the article "a" or "an." Thereafter, in the same claim or in a subsequent dependent claim (more on dependent claims below), the element is referred to as "said" element or "the" element. "Said" has a specific meaning in claim language that might make it easier for a potential infringer or patent attorney to understand. On the other hand, "the" is less formal and may be easier for a judge or jury to understand. Either is acceptable.

"Means for" may also be used to identify elements. For example, ". . . comprising a means for connecting . . ." This is called a "means-plus-function" claim. Another variation of "means for" language could be, for example, ". . . comprising a connecting means . . ." If you use such language, make sure it is clear and well described in the specification.

The relationship between the elements of the invention should be clearly disclosed. Phrases such as "surrounded by," "inserted into," or "connected to," describe the relationship between elements. When deciding the order in which to list the elements and the words used to describe their relationship, ask yourself whether, after reading the claim, if one would be able to easily diagram or draw the invention.

List the elements in the most logical order. Because an invention may consist of several main elements, each in turn comprised of several subelements, organize a claim in an outline using numbers and letters.

### 4. Independent and dependent claims

Claims can be written in either "independent" or "dependent" form. An independent claim stands by itself and does not directly relate to any other claim or claims. Dependent claims, on the other hand, are specifically dependent on another claim. In the case of our one-handed can opener, for example, the first independent claim might be: Claim 1, "A one-handed can opener comprising a handle attached to (a) a turning means and (b) a cutting means." The first dependent claim might be: Claim 2, "Said one-handed can opener of claim 1 wherein said handle is shaped to conform to the human hand."

There are typically between one and three independent claims in a patent application. Additional fees are charged for more than three independent claims. Each independent claim, in turn, has several subordinate or dependent claims that refer to the independent claim. It is also acceptable, for the appropriate fee, to write multiple dependent claims where one claim relates to more than one independent claim. For example, "Said one-handed can opener of claims 1, 5, or 9 wherein . . ."

Not only do independent claims stand alone, but, as you can see from the example of the can opener, they are also broader and more general than dependent claims. Claim 1 will likely be the broadest claim. The broadest claim should describe a generalized version of the invention.

After you have drafted the broadest independent claim, you can then narrow the scope of the invention by drafting several dependent claims, each of which further narrows and more specifically describes the invention. For example, suppose your invention is a new laundry detergent. One element in the broadest independent claim could be a surfactant. In the first dependent claim the surfactant could be narrowed as follows, ". . . wherein said surfactant consists of a long-chain polymer." The next dependent claim could state, ". . . wherein said long-chain polymer consists of a polymer with 20 carbon atoms." The advantage of writing a series of claims that are increasingly narrow and more specific is that should the broadest claim be found to be unpatentable or invalid due to prior art, there is still valuable patent protection due to the language used to describe the narrower dependent claim.

Once you understand and are comfortable with the basic principles of drafting claims, you should find it relatively easy to draft the broadest independent claim followed by several dependent claims. Again, you may want to retain a patent attorney or agent to prepare or review the patent application to make sure it is drafted adequately.

## Rules for Drafting Patent Claims

Follow the rules listed below when drafting patent claims.

1. Make sure all claims are supported by the specification. All claimed elements must be described in the specification exactly the same way they appear in the claims. For example, if you want to recite in the claim that "One element of the invention is a steel rod connecting two pistons," you must include that in the specification.

Review the specification to make sure that all claims are supported.

2. Use only one sentence per claim. This seems self-explanatory, but it cannot be ignored. It is okay to use commas, semicolons, and colons within the claim, although make sure the only period (except for decimal point) in the claim is at the very end.

3. Make sure an element has been named in the claim before modifying or qualifying it. Failure to follow this rule will result in the rejection of the claim for "lack of antecedent basis." More specifically, when you name an element for the first time, say, ". . . a rod" or ". . . an insignia." After this first use, then say ". . . said rod" or ". . . the insignia."

4. Make sure the elements of the claimed invention logically interrelate. A claim must recite an operative combination of elements, not a mere aggregation of elements. The interrelationship between the parts may be structural or functional. Structural relationships between elements are described by words, such as "connected to", "secured to", "near", "adjacent to", "attached to", or "mixed with." For example, ". . . wherein A is connected to B, D is adjacent to C, or E is mixed with F." Functional relationships between elements are described by words such as "to support," "in order to," and "so that it moves." Functional relations between elements could be stated as, ". . . wherein A is positioned to support B. . . ."

5. Use Markush groups if appropriate. A Markush group is defined as an artificial or generic group. There are times when an element of the invention could be made of a number of different materials. These different materials, however, may not neatly fit into a single generic group such as metals or liquids. For example, the handle of the can opener could be made of metal, plastic, or wood. But the PTO generally does not accept claims of ". . . plastic or wood or metal." In such instances, you can create a Markush group. The operative phrase for a Markush group is "selected from the group consisting of." The following example uses a Markush group, "Said can opener wherein said handle is made from material selected from the group consisting of metal, plastic, or wood."

6. If appropriate, use the word "about." The word "about" is acceptable in claims to indicate that a specific number is not absolutely specific, and it helps in obtaining a broader interpretation

of the claim. For example, "comprising about 2% water," "heating said liquid for about 25 minutes," or "a circumference of no more than about 3 feet" effectively use "about" in the claim.

7. Avoid overly precise numbers. The corollary to using the term "about" is that overly precise numbers can be avoided. For example, instead of saying, ". . . mixing said composition for 30 minutes . . . ," say ". . . mixing said composition sufficiently long that said particles are evenly dispersed. . . ."

8. Use functional language when appropriate. Sometimes an element in a claim can best be broadly defined by what it does (e.g., its function). For example, a "means for attaching" could include screws, nails, and adhesives.

9. Be consistent in your use of terms. Once you have used a term in a claim to identify a particular element, use that same term consistently throughout the claims. Define the term as broadly as possible in the description.

10. Avoid unnecessary wordiness. Under Section 112, second paragraph, a claim must be specific enough to particularly point out and distinctly claim the subject matter of your invention. Draft your claims with this rule in mind and you will likely avoid a rejection of "prolixity" by the PTO. Also, do not recite in the claims any elements unless they are critical to practicing the invention.

11. Claim what you plan to sell or license. As obvious as this rule may seem, it is not always followed. When drafting the claims, make sure at least some claims encompass all possible marketable versions, including the version you plan to commercialize. For example, if your invention can be made of any material, be careful not to limit the material from which it can be made in the claims. Try to imagine what other variations your invention might take during its development, and do not preclude those variations by writing claims that are too narrow.

12. Do not hesitate to seek advice or help. No matter how sophisticated you are as an inventor, you may still need help in preparing your patent application. You may want a patent practitioner to review the application before you file it with the PTO. Also, remember that after the application is filed, you can ask the examiner assigned to your case for assistance.

## Preparing Drawings

As recommended earlier, prepare, or have a draftsperson prepare, sketches of the invention even before you begin drafting the specification. These sketches can be submitted as part of the original filing to meet the drawings requirement of the PTO, with the understanding that they will be revised and resubmitted as final drawings to comply with office formalities. These sketches are called "informal" drawings because they may not meet the requirements for "formal" patent drawings.

The PTO has many formalities that must be met for formal drawings. Formal drawings must be on a certain size and type of paper; margins must be a certain width; shading and hatching must be applied using certain methods; and rules for using symbols, legends, and arrows must be followed. These rules are listed in 37 Code of Federal Regulations Sections 1.81–1.85. See also *Guide for the Preparation of Patent Drawings*, published by the PTO and available from the GPO. Unless you are a skilled draftsperson, it is recommended that you hire a professional to make the final, formal drawings.

In addition to drawings to illustrate articles of manufacture, apparatus, or manufacturing equipment, flow charts can also be submitted to illustrate electronic, chemical, or mechanical processes. Flow charts should consist of separate blocks illustrating each step in the process.

While the PTO will accept photographs or color drawings, you are discouraged from submitting them unless absolutely necessary. They are acceptable only if they are submitted in triplicate with an additional fee and a petition requesting their acceptance.

## Completing and Mailing the Application

After you have completed the specification, including at least one claim and the drawings, the application is almost ready to file. As mentioned earlier, in addition to the specification and drawings, there are a number of papers that must also be filed, such as the declaration and filing fee. An appropriate Application Transmittal Letter, Verified Statement of Small Entity Status, Assignment, and an Information Disclosure Statement should also be filed with the patent application.

## The Declaration

The application must be accompanied by a declaration signed by all the inventors. In this document, the inventor(s) declare(s) he or she/ they is/are the sole or joint inventors of the subject matter claimed in the invention. They are also acknowledging a duty to disclose information of which they are aware is material to the examination of the application. This includes (1) all prior art of which they are aware at the time the application is filed or they become aware during the prosecution of the application, and (2) any other information believed to be relevant to a thorough review of the application by the examiner. A sample declaration form is provided at the end of this chapter.

Do not execute the declaration until the application is completed and reviewed by the inventor(s). This rule is strictly maintained by the PTO. Therefore, sign the declaration only after the final changes have been made and you have read the final draft of the application.

## Filing Fee and Small Entity Status

There is a basic fee for filing an application with up to three independent claims and a total of twenty claims. If the number of independent and/or dependent claims exceeds this, then the filing fee increases accordingly. Contact the PTO when you file the application to determine the cost of the filing fees, as the fee schedule for patent applications is regularly updated. Make the check for the total amount payable to Commissioner of Patents and Trademarks. Fees are reduced by 50 percent for applicants who qualify as "small entities." As of October 1, 1997, the regular filing fee for a utility application is $790 and $395 for a small entity. Generally, a small entity is an independent inventor, a business with fewer than five hundred employees, or a nonprofit organization. If you are filing as a small entity, you must also submit a Verified Statement of Small Entity Status. A sample form is included at the end of this chapter.

Filing the patent specification, declaration, and filing fee meets the statutory requirements for a patent application. There are additional documents that you should complete and file as part of your application, if appropriate, with the PTO.

### Application Transmittal Letter

The application should include an Application Transmittal Letter addressed to the Commissioner of Patents and Trademarks. This is a cover letter that lists the contents of the package you are sending to the PTO and includes information such as the names of the inventors, the total number of pages of specification and claims, and the number of sheets of drawings. The letter is also used to calculate the filing fees. See the sample forms at the end of this chapter for an example of an Application Transmittal Letter.

### Assignment

A patent is personal property and may be bought, sold, or licensed for valuable consideration. The patent law provides for the transfer of a patent application by means of a formal Assignment. If you are an individual inventor, chances are you will be looking for a company to make and market your invention. If a company wanted to purchase your patent, you would execute an assignment to transfer ownership. If, at the time the application is filed, you have already agreed to assign the patent to another individual or a company, you can file an Assignment. Have the Assignment notarized to authenticate the document. After filing the Assignment, the PTO will officially record it for a $40 fee. A sample Assignment and Recordation forms are included at the end of this chapter.

### Information Disclosure Statement

An applicant for a patent has a legal obligation to disclose to the PTO any information that is material to the patentability of the invention. To meet this full disclosure requirement, file an Information Disclosure Statement when you file the application. Technically, the Information Disclosure Statement can be filed without a $240 fee up to three months after the application is filed. For ease in dealing with the PTO and while everything is fresh in your mind, prepare and file the statement when filing the patent application.

The Information and Disclosure Statement typically consists of two parts. The first is a form on which all material information is listed. This includes related patents identified during the prior art search including, journal articles and other publications, references cited in related patents, and any commercial activity relating to the invention of which the inventor or anyone involved in preparing the application is aware. Even documents that are not in English should be submitted if they are material to the patentability of the invention. Additionally, a transmittal letter should accompany the form stating that all documents relevant to the application are being submitted. If any documents are not in English, they should briefly be summarized in this transmittal letter. See the forms at the end of this chapter for a sample Information Disclosure Statement and sample Application Transmittal Letter. As a second part of the Information Disclosure Statement, one copy of each reference cited on the form should be submitted.

Deciding what information to disclose to the PTO requires reasoned judgment. There is no need to submit irrelevant or cumulative information, although information that is relevant to patentability must be disclosed. It is best to be overly inclusive. Remember, "When in doubt, do *not* leave it out."

The duty of candor with the PTO is ongoing. If you uncover a piece of prior art after you have filed the application, or if you discover that one embodiment of the invention does not work, you must advise the office before the patent issues. Otherwise, if your patent is granted and it is determined that you withheld material information from the PTO, a court can find your patent unenforceable.

### Petition to Make Special

The PTO will expedite the review of an application under special circumstances. If you want your application to be put at the front of the line, and you can justify this request, you might want to file a Petition to Make Special. A Petition to Make Special may be granted for one of the following reasons:

1. (a) a manufacturer is available to make the invention provided it is patented; (b) or someone is making, using, or selling your invention and you need a granted patent in order to sue; (c) or recombinant DNA is involved; (d) or the invention relates to HIV/AIDS or cancer; and a prior art search was made and an Information Disclosure Statement was submitted to the PTO; or,

2. (a) due to poor health you need expedited review to assure you

will be able to benefit from a patent; (b) the applicant is more than 65 years of age; (c) grant of a patent will enhance the quality of the environment or will result in energy savings; or superconductivity is advanced.

If you are claiming the reasons in item 1 above, you will have to pay a $130 petition fee and file the petition. The Petition to Make Special should be accompanied by a supporting sworn declaration.

### Certificate of Express Mailing

At the beginning or at the end of the Application Transmittal Letter you should prepare a Certificate of Express Mailing. This is a signed statement indicating the date you sent the application by U.S. Express Mail to the PTO. If the patent application is sent to the PTO by U.S. Express Mail and it includes a certificate of express mailing, then the application will receive the filing date that the application was deposited with the postal service. If you hand deliver your patent application to the PTO, a certificate is not necessary and the filing date will be the date on which the application is received by the PTO. The application can also be filed by first-class mail, but the date of receipt by the PTO will be the filing date. A sample Certificate of Express Mailing form is provided at the end of this chapter.

### Self-Addressed Postcard

Enclose a self-addressed, postage-prepaid postcard with the patent application. Write your name, the date, title of the invention, and all documents you are sending to the PTO on the back of the postcard. About two to four weeks after sending the application, you should receive the postcard with a serial number stamped on it. The serial number indicates that the PTO received your application. The returned postcard is evidence of the filing date of your application should a dispute occur.

### The Final Review

If you have followed all the above steps, your application should be ready to file with the PTO. You have accomplished a big job, but do not file the application until you have double-checked it.

Set aside some time to carefully review the application before you mail it. Refer to the patent application checklist at the end of this chapter to make sure you have properly prepared the application. Make sure all signatures are in place, no pages or drawings are missing, and all documents are in proper form.

After you have signed all appropriate documents, make a photocopy of everything to keep in your file. Unfortunately, papers can get lost at the PTO. Your best safeguard against such a mishap is to keep copies of your entire application and forms in a secure place at your office or home.

Place the specification, all related papers, and the filing fee, unfolded, in a large envelope addressed to: Box Patent Application, Assistant Commissioner of Patents and Trademarks, Washington, D.C. 20231. The application can be carried by hand to the PTO. Remember, if you are going to mail the application, you should use only U.S. Express Mail as the filing date will be the date the application is mailed. Furthermore, if you send the application via U.S. Express Mail, the express mail receipt will provide proof of the date the application was sent. Otherwise, the filing date will be the date the application is received by the PTO. This is true even if you use an overnight delivery service such as Federal Express.

## Preparing and Mailing a Design Patent Application

In addition to, or instead of, filing a utility patent application, you may want to file a design patent application. Unlike a utility patent, a design patent protects only the ornamental or aesthetic elements of an invention. Further, design patents do not protect any functional elements of an invention. Design patents can protect, for example, unique bottle shapes, an artistic lamp, an ornamental pin, a watch design, or the grill of a car.

The application for a design patent is much easier to prepare than that for a utility patent. Drawings are the heart of the design patent application, although a short preamble and one claim are also included. The drawings must fully disclose the ornamental features of the invention and should be drawn from a number of views in order to meet full disclosure.

A complete design patent must also include a declaration and the filing fee. You should also file an Information Disclosure Statement and an Application Transmittal Letter identifying everything that you are submitting. Remember, you can file the Information Disclosure

Statement within three months of filing the application without penalty. If applicable, file a Verification Statement of Small Entity Status and a Petition to Make Special.

Submit all these papers just as you would for an application for a utility patent. Remember to include a self-addressed, stamped postcard and send the application by U.S. Express Mail with a Certificate of Express Mail included in the application.

## Provisional Patent Applications

A provisional patent application is much less formal than a regular patent application. Like a regular application, however, a provisional application must adequately and completely describe the invention in accordance with 35 United States Code Section 112, first paragraph. The description does not require all the formalities and sections as a regular patent application. You do not have to file claims, a declaration, or an Information Disclosure Statement with a provisional application. A short Provisional Application Transmittal Letter and the filing fee are the only items that need to be included with a provisional patent application.

Before twelve months have passed after filing a provisional patent application, you can convert it to a regular patent application or file a regular patent application claiming the filing date of the provisional application. This conversion, or filing, requires completing the application so that it meets all the requirements described above for a regular patent application.

### PATENT APPLICATION CHECKLIST

☐ The Specification is complete and has the following components:
   a. Title page, including names of all inventors
   b. References to related applications, if any
   c. Background of the invention
   d. Summary of the invention
   e. Brief description of the drawings, if applicable
   f. Detailed description of the invention

g. Claims, starting on a separate page

h. Abstract, starting on a separate page

☐ All drawings are present, and each sheet of drawings is given a figure number. Your name and address are on the top back of each sheet of formal drawings.

☐ The Declaration Application is completed, signed, and dated in ink by all inventors after having reviewed the specification.

☐ A check or money order payable to the "Commissioner of Patents and Trademarks" for the correct filing fee is enclosed.

☐ If applicable, the Verified Statement of Small Entity Status form is completed, signed, and dated in ink.

☐ If applicable, an Assignment is completed, signed, and dated in ink by all inventors and notarized.

☐ An Information Disclosure Statement and Form PTO-1449 are completed. Copies of all cited references are attached.

☐ If applicable, a Petition to Make Special is completed, signed, and dated in ink.

☐ A properly completed and signed Application Transmittal Letter is enclosed. The letter identifies every document you enclosed to the PTO. A Certificate of Express Mail is included with the letter.

☐ A self-addressed, postage-prepaid postcard, with your name, the mailing date, the title of the invention, and all documents enclosed written on the back.

☐ A large envelope addressed to: Box Patent Application, Assistant Commissioner of Patents and Trademarks, Washington, DC 20231.

## CERTIFICATE OF EXPRESS MAILING PURSUANT TO 37 C.F.R. § 10

I hereby certify that this New Application Transmittal and the documents referred to as enclosed herein are being deposited with the United States Postal Service on this date_____ in an envelope bearing "Express Mail Post Office to Addressee" Mailing Number_____ addressed to the Assistant Commissioner of Patents and Trademarks, Washington, D.C. 20231.

_____
TYPED OR PRINTED NAME OF PERSON MAILING

_____     _____
SIGNATURE OF PERSON MAILING PAPERS                   DATE

Please type a plus sign (+) inside this box → ☐

PTO/SB/05  (8-96)
Approved for use through 9/30/98.  OMB 0651-0032
Patent and Trademark Office: U.S. DEPARTMENT OF COMMERCE
Under the Paperwork Reduction Act of 1995, no persons are required to respond to a collection of information unless it displays a valid OMB control number.

| NEW UTILITY PATENT APPLICATION TRANSMITTAL *(to be used for new applications only)* | Attorney Docket Number | |
| | First Named Inventor | |
| | Total Pages in this Submission | |

## APPLICATION ELEMENTS

*Notice: Checklist items mentioned under **Application Elements** section construct a new utility patent application. Please refer to MPEP Sections 506, 601, (37CFR 1.77, 1.53, 35 USC 111, 112, 113) for detailed explanation regarding completeness of an original patent application.*

1. ☐ Fee Transmittal Form (prescribed filing fee(s))

2. Specification

  ☐ Title of the Invention

  ☐ Cross References to Related Applications *(if applicable)*

  ☐ Statement Regarding Federally-sponsored Research/Development *(if applicable)*

  ☐ Reference to Microfiche Appendix *(if applicable)*

  ☐ Background of the Invention

  ☐ Brief Summary of the Invention

  ☐ Brief Description of the Drawings *(if drawings filed)*

  ☐ Detailed Description

  ☐ Claim or Claims

  ☐ Abstract of the Disclosure

3. ☐ Drawing(s) *(when necessary as prescribed by 35 USC 113)*

4. ☐ Executed Declaration

5. Genetic Sequence Submission *(if applicable, all must be included)*

  ☐ Paper Copy

  ☐ Computer Readable Copy

  ☐ Statement Verifying Identical Paper and Computer Readable Copy

## ACCOMPANYING APPLICATION PARTS

6. ☐ Assignment Papers

7. ☐ Certified Copy of Priority Document(s) *(if foreign priority is claimed)*

8. ☐ Computer Program in Microfiche

9. ☐ English Translation Document *(if applicable)*

10. ☐ Information Disclosure Statement/PTO-1449    ☐ Copies of IDS Citations

11. ☐ Petition Checklist and Accompanying Petition

12. ☐ Preliminary Amendment

13. ☐ Proprietary Information

14. ☐ Return Receipt Postcard

15. ☐ Small Entity Statement

16. ☐ Additional Enclosures *(please identify below):*

### SIGNATURE OF APPLICANT, ATTORNEY, OR AGENT

| Firm *or* Individual name | |
| Signature | |
| Date | |

## FOR OFFICIAL USE ONLY

| Application Number | | Class | | Independent Claims | |
| Date of Receipt | Application Type | GAU | | Total Claims | |
| | Filing Date | Foreign Filing License? | | Drawing Sheets | |
| | Small Entity | Foreign Address? | | Special Handling? | |

| VERIFIED STATEMENT CLAIMING SMALL ENTITY STATUS (37 CFR 1.9(f) & 1.27(b))--INDEPENDENT INVENTOR | Docket Number (Optional) |
|---|---|

Applicant or Patentee: _____

Application or Patent No.: _____

Filed or Issued: _____

Title: _____

As a below named inventor, I hereby declare that I qualify as an independent inventor as defined in 37 CFR 1.9(c) for purposes of paying reduced fees to the Patent and Trademark Office described in:

☐ the specification filed herewith with title as listed above.

☐ the application identified above.

☐ the patent identified above.

I have not assigned, granted, conveyed, or licensed, and am under no obligation under contract or law to assign, grant, convey, or license, any rights in the invention to any person who would not qualify as an independent inventor under 37 CFR 1.9(c) if that person had made the invention, or to any concern which would not qualify as a small business concern under 37 CFR 1.9(d) or a nonprofit organization under 37 CFR 1.9(e).

Each person, concern, or organization to which I have assigned, granted, conveyed, or licensed or am under an obligation under contract or law to assign, grant, convey, or license any rights in the invention is listed below:

☐ No such person, concern, or organization exists.

☐ Each such person, concern, or organization is listed below.

Separate verified statements are required from each named person, concern, or organization having rights to the invention averring to their status as small entities. (37 CFR 1.27)

I acknowledge the duty to file, in this application or patent, notification of any change in status resulting in loss of entitlement to small entity status prior to paying, or at the time of paying, the earliest of the issue fee or any maintenance fee due after the date on which status as a small entity is no longer appropriate. (37 CFR 1.28(b))

I hereby declare that all statements made herein of my own knowledge are true and that all statements made on information and belief are believed to be true; and further that these statements were made with the knowledge that willful false statements and the like so made are punishable by fine or imprisonment, or both, under section 1001 of Title 18 of the United States Code, and that such willful false statements may jeopardize the validity of the application, any patent issuing thereon, or any patent to which this verified statement is directed.

| _____ | _____ | _____ |
| NAME OF INVENTOR | NAME OF INVENTOR | NAME OF INVENTOR |
| _____ | _____ | _____ |
| Signature of inventor | Signature of inventor | Signature of inventor |
| _____ | _____ | _____ |
| Date | Date | Date |

| VERIFIED STATEMENT CLAIMING SMALL ENTITY STATUS (37 CFR 1.9(f) & 1.27(c))--SMALL BUSINESS CONCERN | Docket Number (Optional) |
|---|---|

Applicant or Patentee: _____

Application or Patent No.: _____

Filed or Issued: _____

Title: _____

I hereby declare that I am
☐ the owner of the small business concern identified below:
☐ an official of the small business concern empowered to act on behalf of the concern identified below:

NAME OF SMALL BUSINESS CONCERN _____

ADDRESS OF SMALL BUSINESS CONCERN _____

I hereby declare that the above identified small business concern qualifies as a small business concern as defined in 13 CFR 121.12, and reproduced in 37 CFR 1.9(d), for purposes of paying reduced fees to the United States Patent and Trademark Office, in that the number of employees of the concern, including those of its affiliates, does not exceed 500 persons. For purposes of this statement, (1) the number of employees of the business concern is the average over the previous fiscal year of the concern of the persons employed on a full-time, part-time, or temporary basis during each of the pay periods of the fiscal year, and (2) concerns are affiliates of each other when either, directly or indirectly, one concern controls or has the power to control the other, or a third party or parties controls or has the power to control both.

I hereby declare that rights under contract or law have been conveyed to and remain with the small business concern identified above with regard to the invention described in:

☐ the specification filed herewith with title as listed above.
☐ the application identified above.
☐ the patent identified above.

If the rights held by the above identified small business concern are not exclusive, each individual, concern, or organization having rights in the invention must file separate verified statements averring to their status as small entities, and no rights to the invention are held by any person, other than the inventor, who would not qualify as an independent inventor under 37 CFR 1.9(c) if that person made the invention, or by any concern which would not qualify as a small business concern under 37 CFR 1.9(d), or a nonprofit organization under 37 CFR 1.9(e).

Each person, concern, or organization having any rights in the invention is listed below:
☐ no such person, concern, or organization exists.
☐ each such person, concern, or organization is listed below.

Separate verified statements are required from each named person, concern or organization having rights to the invention averring to their status as small entities. (37 CFR 1.27)

I acknowledge the duty to file, in this application or patent, notification of any change in status resulting in loss of entitlement to small entity status prior to paying, or at the time of paying, the earliest of the issue fee or any maintenance fee due after the date on which status as a small entity is no longer appropriate. (37 CFR 1.28(b))

I hereby declare that all statements made herein of my own knowledge are true and that all statements made on information and belief are believed to be true; and further that these statements were made with the knowledge that willful false statements and the like so made are punishable by fine or imprisonment, or both, under section 1001 of Title 18 of the United States Code, and that such willful false statements may jeopardize the validity of the application, any patent issuing thereon, or any patent to which this verified statement is directed.

NAME OF PERSON SIGNING _____

TITLE OF PERSON IF OTHER THAN OWNER _____

ADDRESS OF PERSON SIGNING _____

SIGNATURE _____ DATE _____

Use the following Certificate of Mailing when the Information Disclosure Statement is filed by first class mail:

## CERTIFICATE OF MAILING PURSUANT TO 37 C.F.R. SECTION 1.8

I hereby certify that this Information Disclosure Statement is being deposited with the United States Postal Service as First-Class Mail in an envelope addressed to Commissioner of Patents and Trademarks, Washington, D.C. 20231 on

_____.

_____

DATE OF DEPOSIT

_____

NAME OF APPLICANT OR REGISTERED REPRESENTATIVE

_____

SIGNATURE

## TRANSMITTAL FOR INFORMATION DISCLOSURE STATEMENT

IN THE UNITED STATES PATENT AND TRADEMARK OFFICE

Applicant:                           Examiner:

Serial No.:                          Art Unit:

Filing Date:

Title:

TRANSMITTAL FOR INFORMATION DISCLOSURE STATEMENT
BEFORE PAYMENT OF ISSUE FEE

Commissioner of Patents and Trademarks

Box DD

Washington, D.C. 20231

Sir:

Transmitted herewith for filing and pursuant to 37 C.F.R. § 1.97 is an Information Disclosure Statement.

In order to secure consideration of this Information Disclosure Statement, one or more of the following, if required, is also enclosed:

Promptness Certification

☐ Please charge Deposit Account No._____ in the amount of $_____ (amount in § 1.17(p)) to cover the submission fee.

☐ Enclosed is a check in the amount of $_____ (amount in § 1.17(p)) to cover the submission fee.

☐ Petition and check in the amount of $_____ (amount in § 1.17(i)(1)) to cover the petition fee.

In the event that 37 C.F.R. § 1.97(c) applies and the Examiner is not satisfied that the Promptness Certification meets the requirements of 37 C.F.R. § 1.97(e), or in any other event remediable by a fee, the following is authorized, if indicated:

Please credit any overpayment or charge any additional fees to Deposit Account No._____ of the undersigned.

Respectfully submitted,

Date:

Direct Communications To:

# INFORMATION DISCLOSURE STATEMENT

IN THE UNITED STATES PATENT AND TRADEMARK OFFICE

Applicant:                                    Examiner:
Serial No.:                                   Art Unit:
Filing Date:                                  Title:

INFORMATION DISCLOSURE STATEMENT UNDER 37 C.F.R. § 1.97

Commissioner of Patents and Trademarks
Washington, D.C. 20231

Sir:

Please find, pursuant to 37 C.F.R. § 1.98(a)(1), the enclosed Form PTO-1449, which contains a list of all patents, publications, or other items that have come to the attention of one or more of the individuals designated in 37 C.F.R. § 1.56(c). While no representation is made that any of these references may be "prior art" within the meaning of that term under 35 U.S.C. §§ 102 or 103, the enclosed list of references is disclosed so as to fully comply with the duty of disclosure set forth in 37 C.F.R. § 1.56.

Moreover, while no representation is made that a specific search of office files or patent office records has been conducted or that no better art exists, the undersigned believes that the enclosed art is the closest to the claimed invention (taken in its entirety) of which the undersigned is presently aware, and no art which is closer to the claimed invention (taken in its entirety) has been knowingly withheld.

In accordance with 37 C.F.R. §§ 1.97 and 1.98, a copy of each of the listed references or relevant portion thereof is also enclosed.

In accordance with 37 C.F.R. § 1.98(c), all English translations within the possession, custody, control, or availability of anyone designated in 37 C.F.R. § 1.56(c) of each non-English reference, if any, are also enclosed.

### [if applicable]
Statement of Relevance of References Listed Unaccompanied
by English Translation Under 37 C.F.R. § 1.98(a)(3)

In accordance with 37 C.F.R. § 1.98(a)(3), the following concise explanation of the relevance of each listed reference that is either not in the English language or unaccompanied by a translation into English is provided.

Since all listed references are either in the English language or are accompanied by a translation into English, no concise explanation of relevance is required under 37 C.F.R. § 1.98(a)(3).

**[if applicable]**
Statement of Cumulative References Under 37 C.F.R. § 1.98(c)

The following listed references are not enclosed because, under 37 C.F.R. § 1.98(c), they are substantially cumulative of the reference:

**[if applicable]**
Statement of References Previously Disclosed Under 37 C.F.R. § 1.98(d)

The following listed references are not enclosed because, under 37 C.F.R. § 1.98(d), they were previously cited by or submitted to the Office in the prior application, which is relied upon for an earlier filing date under 35 U.S.C. § 120.

Respectfully submitted,

Date:

Direct Communications To:

Sheet_____ of_____

| FORM PTO-1449 U.S. DEPARTMENT OF COMMERCE<br>PATENT AND TRADEMARK OFFICE<br>INFORMATION DISCLOSURE<br>STATEMENT BY APPLICANT<br>(Use several sheets if necessary)<br><br>(Rev. 2-32) | ATTY. DOCKET NO. | SERIAL NO. |
|---|---|---|
| | APPLICANT | |
| | FILING DATE | GROUP |

## U.S. PATENT DOCUMENTS

| EXAMINER INITIAL | DOCUMENT NUMBER | | | | | | | DATE | NAME | CLASS | SUB-CLASS | FILING DATE IF APPROPRIATE |
|---|---|---|---|---|---|---|---|---|---|---|---|---|
| | | | | | | | | | | | | |
| | | | | | | | | | | | | |
| | | | | | | | | | | | | |
| | | | | | | | | | | | | |
| | | | | | | | | | | | | |
| | | | | | | | | | | | | |
| | | | | | | | | | | | | |
| | | | | | | | | | | | | |

## FOREIGN PATENT DOCUMENTS

| EXAMINER INITIAL | DOCUMENT NUMBER | | | | | | | DATE | COUNTRY | CLASS | SUB-CLASS | TRANSLATION YES | NO |
|---|---|---|---|---|---|---|---|---|---|---|---|---|---|
| | | | | | | | | | | | | | |
| | | | | | | | | | | | | | |
| | | | | | | | | | | | | | |
| | | | | | | | | | | | | | |
| | | | | | | | | | | | | | |
| | | | | | | | | | | | | | |
| | | | | | | | | | | | | | |
| | | | | | | | | | | | | | |

## OTHER DOCUMENTS (including author, title, date, pertinent pages, etc.)

| | |
|---|---|
| | |
| | |
| | |
| EXAMINER | DATE CONSIDERED |

EXAMINER: Initial if citation considered, whether or not citation is in conformance with MPEP 609; draw line through citation if not in conformance and not considered. Include copy of this form with next communication to applicant.

## COMBINED DECLARATION AND POWER OF ATTORNEY FOR ORIGINAL APPLICATION

As a below named inventor, I hereby declare that:

(1) my residence, post office address, and citizenship are stated below next to my name; and that

(2) I verily believe I am an original, first, and joint inventor of the improvement in: **[Title of Invention]**

☐ described and claimed in the attached specification which is attached hereto.

☐ was filed on_____ as Application Serial No._____ and was ☐

☐ amended on_____.

I hereby state that I have reviewed and understand the contents of the above identified specification, including the claims, as amended by any amendment referred to above.

I acknowledge the duty to disclose information which is material to the patentability of this application in accordance with the provisions of 37 C.F.R. § 1.56.

I hereby claim foreign priority benefits pursuant to 35 U.S.C. § 119 from any foreign application(s) listed below and have also identified below any foreign application(s) for patent or inventor's certificate which have a filing date prior to that of the application from which priority is claimed.

Prior Foreign Application(s) (if any):

| NUMBER | COUNTRY | FILING DATE | PRIORITY CLAIMED |
|--------|---------|-------------|------------------|
|        |         |             |                  |

I hereby claim the benefit under 35 U.S.C. § 120 from any United States application(s) listed below and, insofar as the subject matter of each of the claims of this application is not disclosed in the prior United States application in the manner provided by the first paragraph of 35 U.S.C. § 112, I acknowledge the duty to disclose material information as defined in 37 C.F.R. § 1.56 which occurred between the filing date of the prior application and the national or PCT international filing date of this application:

| APPLICATION SERIAL NO. | FILING DATE | STATUS (PATENTED, PENDING, ABANDONED) |
|------------------------|-------------|----------------------------------------|
|                        |             |                                        |

I hereby appoint the following attorney(s) and or agent(s) to prosecute this application and to transact all business in the Patent and Trademark Office connected therewith:

Address all telephone calls to_____ at telephone number_____

Address all correspondence to:

I hereby declare that all statements made herein of my own knowledge are true and that all statements made on information and belief are believed to be true, and, further, that these statements were made with knowledge that willful false statements and the like are punishable by fine or imprisonment, or both, pursuant to 18 U.S.C. § 1001 and that such willful false statements may jeopardize the validity of the application or any patent issued thereon.

Full Name of Inventor:

Signature of Inventor:

Date:

Residence:

Citizenship:

Post Office Address:

| | |
|---|---|
| **RECORDATION FORM COVER SHEET**<br>**PATENTS ONLY** | FORM PTO-1595<br>U.S. DEPARTMENT OF COMMERCE<br>PATENT AND TRADEMARK OFFICE |

To the Honorable Commissioner of Patents and Trademarks: Please record the attached original documents or copy thereof.

| 1. Name of conveying party(ies): | 2. Name and address of receiving party(ies):<br><br>Name:<br><br>Internal Address: |
|---|---|
| 3. Nature of conveyance:<br><br>   Assignment<br>   Merger<br>   Security Agreement<br>   Change of Name<br>   Other _____<br><br>Execution date: | Street Address:<br><br>City:             State:      ZIP:<br><br>Additional name(s) & address(es) attached? Yes  No |

4. Application number(s) or patent number(s):

If this document is being filed together with a new application, the execution date of the application is:

| A. Patent Application No(s) | B. Patent No(s) |
|---|---|

                            Additional numbers attached? Yes  No

| 5. Name and address of party to whom correspondence<br>   concerning document should be mailed<br><br>Name:<br><br>Internal Address:<br><br>Street Address:<br><br>City:        State:     ZIP: | 6. Total number of applications and patents involved: 1 |
|---|---|
| | 7. Total fee (37 CFR 3.41)...............................$40.00<br><br>   Enclosed<br><br>   Authorized to be charged to deposit account |
| | 8. Deposit account number:<br><br>(Attach duplicate copy of this page if paying by deposit account.) |

9. Statement and signature. To the best of my knowledge and belief, the foregoing information is true and correct and any attached copy is a true copy of the original document.

_____    _____    _____
NAME OF PERSON SIGNING                  SIGNATURE                           DATE

Total number of pages including cover sheet, attachments, and documents:

Mail documents to be recorded with required cover sheet information to: Commissioner of Patents & Trademarks, Box Assignments, Washington, D.C. 20231

Use the following Certificate of Mailing when the Assignment Recordation is filed by First-Class Mail:

## CERTIFICATE OF MAILING PURSUANT TO 37 C.F.R. SECTION 1.8

I hereby certify that this Assignment Recordation is being deposited with the United States Postal Service as First-Class Mail in an envelope addressed to Commissioner of Patents and Trademarks, Washington, D.C. 20231 on

_____

DATE OF DEPOSIT


_____

NAME OF APPLICANT OR REGISTERED REPRESENTATIVE


_____

SIGNATURE

| ASSIGNMENT OF APPLICATION | Docket Number (Optional) |
|---|---|

Whereas, I, _____ of _____, hereafter

referred to as applicant, have invented certain new and useful improvements in _____

_____

☐ for which an application for a United States Patent was filed on _____,
Application Number _____/_____.

☐ for which an application for a United States Patent was executed on _____, and

Whereas, _____ of _____ herein referred to

"assignee" whose post office address is _____ is de-

sirous of acquiring the entire right, title and interest in the same;

Now, therefore, in consideration of the sum of _____ dollars ($_____), the receipt whereof is ac-

knowledged, and other good and valuable consideration, I, the applicant, by these presents do sell, assign

and transfer unto said assignee the full and exclusive right to the said invention in the United States and the

entire right, title and interest in and to any and all Patents which may be granted therefor in the United States,

I hereby authorize and request the Commissioner of Patents and Trademarks to issue said United States

Patent to said assignee, of the entire right, title, and interest in and to the same, for his sole use and behoof;

and for the use and behoof of his legal representatives, to the full end of the term for which said Patent may

be granted, as fully and entirely as the same would have been held by me had this assignment and sale not

been made.

Executed this _____ day of _____, 19_____,

at _____.

_____
(Signature)

State of _____ ) SS:
County of _____ )
Before me personally appeared said _____
and acknowledged the foregoing instrument to be his free act and deed this _____
day of _____, 19_____.

**Seal**

_____
(Notary Public)

# Prosecuting a Patent Application in the U.S. Patent and Trademark Office

I N CHAPTER 8 you learned how to draft and file an application for a United States patent. Chapter 9 explains the steps involved in the application review and examination process. This review and examination process is typically referred to as "patent prosecution." The complete process, from filing the application to the granting of a patent, takes about two years.

## Processing the Application

When a patent application arrives at the PTO, the Applications Branch examines the papers to make sure the required parts of the application have been submitted. The application is then assigned a filing date and a serial number and is put in a folder called a "file wrapper." The application serial number is stamped on the self-addressed postcard and then returned to you. A formal filing receipt will be prepared and mailed to you.

A filing receipt is a document from the PTO that officially acknowledges that the application has met the minimal filing requirements.

The filing receipt includes the following: the serial number assigned to the application, the filing date of the application, the group art unit to which the application has been assigned, the number of sheets of drawings, the number of claims, the number of independent claims, the names and addresses of the inventors, the words "Small Entity" (if applicable), and the words "Foreign Filing License Granted" (assuming the invention is not a classified military secret).

When you receive the filing receipt, check it for accuracy. Make sure that the filing date is the date that you express mailed or hand delivered the application, that all the names are spelled correctly, and that there are no typographical errors. If the filing receipt has errors, write a letter correcting them and send it to the Commissioner of Patents and Trademarks, Washington, D.C. 20231, Attn: Applications Branch. Always provide the following information at the beginning of your correspondence when writing to the PTO: application serial number, filing date, names of all inventors, title of application, name of examiner, and number of assigned art unit. The PTO uses the application serial number to track the application. The serial number is the best way to identify the application when communicating with the PTO.

If the patent application does not include all the required parts, you will be sent a Notice of Missing Parts. This paper identifies material that is necessary for a complete application, such as the signed Declaration or the filing fee. Although the incomplete application will be given a filing date and a serial number, the missing parts must be sent to the PTO within the time specified on the notice (generally one month, but extensions of time can be obtained for a fee). Remember to include a self-addressed, postage-prepaid postcard and the appropriate Certificate of Mailing with everything you send to the PTO.

After all the required parts of the patent application have been received by the PTO, the filing receipt discussed earlier will be issued and the application will be examined in due course.

## The First Office Action

After the application is processed by the Applications Branch, it is forwarded to the appropriate examination group and assigned to a patent examiner. The examiner reviews the application for compliance with PTO formalities and the Patent Statute and regulations. This review includes a prior art search of earlier patents and publications to determine whether the claims are novel and unobvious. The examiner will then prepare and mail a report called an Office Action, setting forth his or her opinion of the application. Attached to the Office Action are copies of the relevant prior art uncovered in the examiner's search. The Office Action identifies which claims, if any, are acceptable or "allowed" and which are unacceptable or "rejected." The Office Action lists reasons for rejected claims. The Office Action also indicates if there are any other problems with the application. The first Office Action is usually received about six to twelve months after the application is filed. You are typically given three months to respond to the Office Action, and this time period can be extended to six months by paying the required fee.

It is not unusual for the examiner to reject all the claims in the first Office Action, however, this is not the end of prosecution. Examiners are under pressure to review cases quickly. Therefore, they may reject all the claims in order to force you to more clearly explain the essence of your invention and its unique features and distinguish it from the prior art.

Although most Office Actions are self-explanatory, be sure you fully understand the reasons for the examiner's objections and rejections. If you are having trouble understanding an Office Action, reread it. Then, read it a third time, if necessary. If you simply cannot figure out what the examiner means, call him or her for clarification.

It is also possible, but not likely, that upon initial review the examiner will find that all the claims are patentable and the application is acceptable as submitted. If so, the examiner will issue a Notice of Allowance instead of an Office Action. If you receive a Notice of Allowance, all that remains is to attend to any formal matters and to pay the issue fee.

## Calculating the Response Date

When you receive the first Office Action, the date it was mailed will be typed near the top right. This date is important because it is the date from which the time period to respond to the Office Action is calculated. Failure to respond to an Office Action within the allotted time can result in the abandonment of the application.

The period for response is indicated on the Office Action and is normally three months from the mailing date of the action. Extensions of time from one, two, three, or four months can be obtained if requested by petition and by payment of the required fee. The maximum time to respond to an Office Action is six months from the mailing date of the action. This includes the three months from the mailing date plus up to three additional months. If the calculated date for responding falls on a weekend or a holiday, you can respond on the following business day. The date of your response will be the date you deposit it with the U.S. Postal Service, if you include the appropriate certificate of first-class or express mailing with the response. Otherwise, the date of the response will be the date it is received by the PTO.

If you respond after the third month but before the sixth month, you must submit a Petition for Extension of Time before or at the time you submit your response. This petition is typically a short form requesting a one-, two-, or three-month extension—whichever is applicable. You must also submit an extension fee with the petition. Check the fee schedule in the Appendix and with the PTO for changes. A Petition for Extension of Time is always granted, provided it is properly completed and accompanied by the correct fee. A sample Petition for Extension of Time is provided at the end of this chapter.

Check carefully each paper you receive from the PTO to determine when it is due. Some papers, such as a the Notice of Missing Parts, may require a response within one month instead of the usual three months. Again, you can ask for an extension of up to five months for a maximum of six months.

## Preparing an Amendment and Response

Before responding to an Office Action, review it carefully, including all the prior art cited by the examiner. If you find you do not have all the prior art or pages of the Office Action, contact the examiner and ask that the missing materials be sent to you as soon as possible. If the Office Action is not clear to you, discuss it with the examiner to make certain you fully understand it.

Next, categorize the examiner's remarks. They should normally fit into the following categories: (1) objections based on formalities, such as misspellings or trademarks, (2) rejection of the specification under 35 U.S.C. § 112, first paragraph, (3) rejection of claims in view of 35 U.S.C. § 112, second paragraph, and (4) rejection of one or more claims based on prior art as listed under 35 U.S.C. § 102 and/ or § 103. If there are rejections based on other sections of the Patent Statute, put those in yet another category. Using this technique, it will be much easier to respond to what may at first appear to be an overwhelming number of objections and rejections. Decide how you will respond to each objection and rejection and prepare your response. Your response should be complete, accurate, and persuasive, as it is the key to showing the examiner that the invention is patentable.

Perhaps the best way to respond to the first Office Action is to revise the specification and claims to overcome the examiner's objections and rejections, provided that the revised claims adequately cover you invention. These revisions are called "amendments" and they will be submitted with your remarks in a document called an Amendment and Response. See the sample Amendment and Response form at the end of this chapter.

The Amendment and Response typically begins by stating:

> This Amendment and Response is submitted in response to the Examiner's Office Action dated_____. Please amend the above identified application as follows: . . .

Next, amend the specification as necessary to respond to the Office Action; this includes correcting formal objections such as typographical and spelling errors. In addition, the specification should be amended if the examiner rejects it based on failure to comply with 35 U.S.C. § 112, first paragraph, requiring an adequate description of the invention. Remember, no new matter can be added to the application, but you can usually overcome a rejection under § 112, first paragraph, by adding a few words of clarification without adding new matter.

Here are some ways to amend the specification in a patent application:

- To replace a word or words in the specification, state, "On page_____, line_____, change 'front' to —side—."
- To remove a word, state, "On page_____, line_____, delete 'sliding.'"
- To insert one or more words, state, "On page_____, line_____, after the word 'rigid' insert—or flexible—."
- Use the methods described above to replace, remove, or add large portions of text such as a paragraph or page.

The next step is to make appropriate amendments to the claims. Amending the claims may require narrowing them to overcome prior art or revising them to more clearly describe the claimed invention. A new element or component may be added to the claims to overcome an anticipation rejection under 35 U.S.C. § 102(b). Other limitations (such as amounts, forms, use, or mode of operation) may be added to the claims to get around an obviousness rejection based on 35 U.S.C. § 103. Your goal should be to overcome the examiner's rejections without narrowing the claims any more than necessary. You may want to speak to a patent attorney or patent agent about the best way to amend the claims. You can also ask the examiner to assist you in amending the claims.

Amend the claims using one of the following techniques:

- If you are cancelling or adding no more than five words, use the same format used to amend the specification. For example, state, "Claim_____, line___, change 'immobile' to —flexible—."
- If more than five words are being added, rewrite the entire claim, including the new language, then bracket the language to be deleted and underline the added language. For example:

Claim 1 (Amended)

A method for relieving arthritic pain comprising topically applying [an anti-inflammatory composition selected from the group consisting of ibuprofen, aspirin, and salicylic acid.] about 500 milligrams of ibuprofen.

- You can cancel the claim you want to amend and substitute it with a new claim; the new claim would be given the next unused claim number. For example, if you have ten claims, you can amend claim 1 by stating the following:

Cancel claim 1. Add new claim 11, as follows:

—11. A composition for relieving arthritic pain comprising about 500 milligrams of ibuprofen, whereby said ibuprofen is topically applied.—

It may be easier for the examiner to review claims amended according to this technique, and it is recommended you use this technique if you are adding more than five words.

After you have amended the specification and claims, begin the Remarks section of the Amendment and Response, preferably on a new page. In this section, respond directly to all the examiner's objections and rejections. The best way to do this is to identify each of the examiner's objections and rejections and repeat it by stating, "The examiner has objected to the specification under §112, first paragraph, because . . .". Then, respond to this objection or rejection by pointing out how the specification has been amended. If you have chosen not to offer an amendment in response to the objection, explain why an amendment is not needed. Repeat this process for every rejection and objection made by the examiner. Follow these guidelines in preparing the Amendment and Response:

- Type the response in English, preferably double-spaced, on letter-, legal-, or A4-size paper. Use the same margins required in the specification.
- Make sure you follow the format described above to amend the specification and claims.
- Always be polite and do not get personal with the examiner. The Amendment and Response is addressed to the Commissioner of Patents and Trademarks, not specifically to the examiner. Do not say, "you said"; say, "the examiner has

stated . . . ," or "Claim 1 has been rejected because. . . ." Similarly, always refer to yourself as "the Applicant."

- Refer to the amendments when responding to a rejection, if appropriate. State, for example, "In response to the examiner's rejection, claim 1 has been amended to claim the anti-inflammatory ibuprofen."

- If you have to convince the examiner that your invention is not obvious in view of the prior art, try the following arguments where applicable:
  1. the results achieved by your invention are "unexpected";
  2. your invention has been highly commercially successful;
  3. those skilled in the art were never able to solve the problem solved by your invention; the invention meets a long-felt, previously unmet need;
  4. the prior art references teach away from your invention, e.g., they state or imply that your invention would not work;
  5. while your invention may combine two known compounds, elements, or steps, the result achieved by your invention is "synergistic." In other words, the whole is greater than the sum of its parts;
  6. the prior art reference is from a different field, and is "nonanalogous art";
  7. the art cited by the examiner is inoperative; and
  8. the invention has been recognized by others in the industry as evidenced by awards, attempts to license, and copying.

- Consider submitting an affidavit under 37 C.F.R. § 132 providing factual support for your remarks. For example, an affidavit might be appropriate (1) to present facts relevant to the operability of your invention that might not be in the specification, (2) to present experimental results that clarify the uniqueness of your invention, and (3) to present supporting evidence that your invention has had impressive commercial success.

Your remarks and arguments should be as clear and concise as possible. After you have provided remarks for each objection and rejection, conclude by stating, "For the foregoing reasons, Applicant respectfully submits that the claims (as amended) are drawn to novel subject matter, patentably distinct from the art of record and allowable in form. Favorable reconsideration and a Notice of Allowance are respectfully requested."

Finally, close your response with "Respectfully submitted," and sign and date the response. Type your address and telephone number below your name in case the examiner needs to contact you.

The Amendment and Response can be sent to the PTO by United States regular, first-class, or express mail, or by facsimile. Prepare a cover Transmittal Form to send to the PTO with any documents you are submitting. A sample Transmittal Form is given at the end of this chapter. If you use U.S. mail, include a self-addressed, postage-prepaid postcard. Make sure you put a Certificate of Mailing, Certificate of Express Mailing, or Certificate of Facsimile Transmission, whichever is relevant, on each document you send to the PTO.

## Amending the Drawings

The Office Action may also include objections to the drawings, especially if you submitted informal drawings when you filed the application. Drawing amendments are submitted as a separate document and routed to the PTO draftsperson for review and approval. However, acknowledge the drawing rejections to the examiner in the Remarks section, stating that the objections are noted and will be corrected separately. Frequently, drawings are not corrected and filed as formal drawings until after a Notice of Allowance has been received. At that time, make sure you submit drawings promptly to allow time for further corrections if necessary.

## Interviewing the Examiner

After you receive the first Office Action it may also be helpful to call the examiner to arrange a face-to-face meeting, technically called an "interview." Interviews normally occur in the examiner's office at the PTO in Crystal City, Virginia. Interviews with the examiner can also be conducted over the telephone, but in-person interviews are usually more effective in getting claims allowed. If you decide to interview the examiner, make your request by telephoning the examiner. The examiner's phone number should be at the end of the Office Action.

Come to the interview fully prepared. Be familiar with the examiner's objections and rejections and be prepared to discuss them. Draft proposed amendments to the claims for the examiner's review, which you can offer to send to the examiner before you meet. If appropriate, bring the invention with you for demonstration purposes.

An in-person interview can greatly facilitate prosecution of the application. An interview will give you a chance to explain and perhaps demonstrate your invention, and it will give the examiner a chance to meet and personally interact with you. Generally, examiners welcome interviews since so much of their time is spent working alone in a small office. Meeting with an examiner in an open and nonadversarial way allows you to establish personal rapport that can go a long way in getting a patent granted.

## Restriction Requirements

Even before you receive the first substantive Office Action, the examiner may issue a Restriction Requirement and/or a Request for an Election of Species. The examiner will issue a Restriction Requirement if he or she believes that more than one invention is claimed in the application. For example, if you have claimed two different compositions of matter, e.g., a new plastic and a new steel, the examiner may issue a Restriction Requirement stating that the application is to be restricted to a single invention. You must then choose between the claims directed to plastic or the claims directed to steel and advise the examiner which set of claims you wish to continue to prosecute. The rest of the claims can be prosecuted in a divisional application at a later date without losing your original filing date.

You can respond to a Restriction Requirement by stating, "In response to the Restriction Requirement, Applicant elects, with traverse, claims_____ through_____." Try to convince the examiner that the restriction requirement is not reasonable, and that all claims are directed to a single unitary invention. It is not likely you will successfully overcome a restriction requirement. But stating that you are electing certain claims "with traverse" will allow you to challenge the requirement for restriction and document in the record that you do not necessarily agree with the examiner.

A Request for an Election of Species will be issued if various species in a generic invention are claimed. This is often the case in an application relating to a composition that discloses various Markush groups of components. For example, you may have a claim for a composition comprising ". . . component C, wherein C is selected from the group consisting of x, y, and z." Because the examiner will only examine a limited number of species, he or she may require you to elect only one species from the group for examination.

You can respond to a Request for an Election of Species as follows, "In response to the Examiner's requirement for an election of species, Applicant elects with traverse the following species:_____."

The examiner will not begin a substantive review of the application and issue the first Office Action until your response to the Restriction Requirement and/or the Request for an Election of Species is received. Therefore, respond to these requests as soon as possible in order to begin substantive prosecution of the application.

## Subsequent Office Actions and Final Rejection

After the examiner has reviewed your Amendment and Response, he or she will allow all, some, or none of the claims. The examiner will issue a Notice of Allowance if all of the claims are allowed. If all the claims are not allowed, another Office Action will be issued.

The second Office Action is usually a Final Office Action, and will be indicated on the document. There are several ways you can respond to a Final Office Action, such as (1) amending the claims and filing an Amendment and Response After Final Rejection, (2) filing a Response After Final Rejection and trying to convince the examiner to allow the claims without amending them, (3) appealing the examiner's rejections to the Board of Patent Appeals and

Interferences or petitioning the Commissioner of Patents and Trademarks, whichever applies, (4) refiling the application as a continuation application and continuing the prosecution, or (5) calling it quits and deciding to abandon the application. You can also elect to first respond and then, depending on the outcome of the response, exercise options three, four, or five.

## Amendment After Final Rejection

An amendment and/or response after final rejection should have a heading of, for example, Amendment and Response under 37 C.F.R. § 1.116 or Response After Final under 37 C.F.R. § 1.116.

The first sentence of the document might state, "In response to the Office Action dated _____, Applicant respectfully requests entry of this Amendment and Response pursuant to 37 C.F.R. § 1.116." The rest of the document is prepared the same way you prepared the previous Amendment and Response.

Amend the specification and claims as needed to overcome the rejections of the examiner. If you are amending a claim that has already been amended, rewrite the claim as it was previously amended, and then indicate deletions and insertions of material as described earlier. For example, "Claim 1 (Twice Amended): A method for relieving arthritic pain comprising topically applying about [500] 600 milligrams of ibuprofen."

In the Remarks section, respond to every objection and rejection the examiner has made. Try to convince the examiner that his or her conclusions are erroneous and that you have shown a prima facie case of patentability of the invention.

When you are "under final rejection," the clock is ticking. You have only six months to submit an "Amendment After Final," wait for a response from the examiner, and, if necessary, either begin the appeal process or refile the application. Therefore, to expedite review of this Amendment and Response, write "Response under 37 C.F.R. § 1.116—expedited procedure—Examining Group No._____" in the upper right portion of the first page. Highlight this notice or write it with a red pen. Also, address the envelope to: Box AF, Commissioner of Patents and Trademarks, Washington, D.C. 20231. Don't forget the self-addressed, postage-prepaid postcard identifying the documents you have sent, along with the serial number of the application and the mailing date.

After the examiner has reviewed these documents you will be notified. If the examiner has, at last, decided to allow the claims, you will receive a Notice of Allowance as described below. If the case is not allowed, you should still have time to either file an Appeal or a Petition or refile the case to continue prosecution. And, of course, you can give up on patenting the invention and abandon the application.

Which option you exercise depends on your answers to the following questions. In view of the prior art, is the invention patentable? Does the examiner understand the claimed invention? Are the examiner's rejections reasonable? Has the examiner incorrectly applied the Patent Statute in rejecting the claims? How important is the patent? If I refile the application, is it likely the claims will eventually be allowed without going through the appeal process? How likely is it that I will prevail on appeal? Is it cost-effective to continue prosecution by refiling or appealing? If I appeal, am I willing to wait two years or more for a decision?

## Appeals and Petitions

Rejection of claims for substantive reasons (e.g., rejection under 35 U.S.C. § 102 and/or § 103) are appealable to the Board of Patent Appeals and Interferences. You must file a Notice of Appeal within the prescribed or extended time period to start the appeal process. A Notice of Appeal must be filed within six months of receiving a Final Office Action. An Appeal Brief must then be filed within two months after filing the Notice of Appeal, but this period can be extended to a maximum of six months. See the forms at the end of this chapter for a sample Notice of Appeal.

An Appeal Brief must comply with certain formalities. The required sections of an Appeal Brief, itemized in 37 C.F.R. § 1.192(c), are (1) a statement of real part in interest, (2) a statement of related appeals and interferences, (3) a statement of the status of the claims, (4) a statement of the status of the amendments, (5) a summary of the invention, (6) issues for review, (7) a grouping of claims, (8) an argument, (9) a conclusion, (10) your signature, and

(11) a copy of the claims under appeal attached as an appendix. The examiner will review the Appeal Brief and file an answer. You may then file a Reply Brief in response to the examiner's answer.

Eventually, the Board of Appeals and Patent Interferences will review your case. You may request an oral hearing at which you will be given an opportunity to argue your case. If the board disagrees with the examiner, it will issue a written decision, which should eventually result in an allowance of the case. If the board upholds the examiner's rejection(s), you will also be so advised in a written decision.

The Board of Appeals and Patent Interferences is not the "court of last resort." If the application is important enough, you can appeal to the Court of Appeals for the Federal Circuit or the Federal District Court for the District of Columbia and up to the U.S. Supreme Court if there is a legal basis. This is an expensive and time-consuming process that will almost certainly require the assistance of legal counsel.

Objections to applications based on noncompliance with formalities are petitionable to the Commissioner of the Patent and Trademark Office. Generally, petitionable matters are those relating to practice and procedure of the PTO. Petition the commissioner as soon as possible after the occurrence of the petitionable event. Make sure the petition sets forth all the relevant facts and, if necessary, is accompanied by one or more declarations setting forth supporting evidence.

## Refiling the Application

An alternative to appealing the examiner's rejections to the board is to refile the application as a "continuation" application. A continuation application retains the original application filing date and is prosecuted in much the same way as the original application. An advantage of refiling is that you may have two more chances to overcome the examiner's rejections by further amending the application and/or presenting arguments to the examiner as to why the claims should be allowed. A disadvantage of refiling is that you must pay another filing fee and prosecution of the application is extended.

Note that, in addition to refiling an application in order to overcome rejections, patent applications can be refiled for other reasons. The first case that is filed in a series of applications is called the "parent" application. Your original parent application, however, may have several generations of offspring. For example, if your original application was subject to a restriction requirement because it claimed two different inventions, you have the right to refile the claims you did not originally elect by filing a second application. This second application is called a "divisional" application. Even though you file the divisional application after filing the original application, it is still entitled to the original filing date.

Or perhaps after filing the parent application you have discovered a way to improve the invention by adding a new element. Remember, you cannot add new matter to an application after it has been filed. What you can do, however, is file a "continuation-in-part application." As its name implies, part of this second application is identical to and can claim priority on the first application, while the remainder of the application contains the new matter discovered after the parent was filed.

## Notice of Allowance

When the examiner is satisfied that the claims are in allowable form, he or she will issue a Notice of Allowance. When you receive a Notice of Allowance, make any required corrections to the drawings, specification, and claims, and then carefully review them to make sure everything is correct. If you notice any errors in the application, you can correct them provided they do not alter the substance of the application.

To correct errors, submit an Amendment Pursuant to 37 C.F.R. § 1.312. The Amendment should begin with a statement such as, "Applicant submits this Amendment Pursuant to 37 C.F.R. § 1.312. Applicant respectfully requests the above application be amended as follows: . . . ." Then, amend the specification and claims as described earlier. Finally, state in your remarks that the amendments do not alter the substance of the application. Sign and date the amendment and include your telephone number and address at the bottom of the amendment.

The Notice of Allowance will state that you have three months to respond and pay the issue fee. The three-month time period is nonextendable. The amount of the issue fee will be indicated on the Notice of Allowance and is currently $1,320 ($660 for a small entity). Approximately three to six months after you pay the issue fee, you will receive an Issue Notification Form, stating the serial number assigned to your patent and the date it will issue. The formal Letters Patent will be sent to you on that day. Patents always issue at noon on Tuesdays.

Please type a plus sign (+) inside this box → ☐

PTO/SB/21 (10-96)
Approved for use through 10/31/99. OMB 0651-0031
Patent and Trademark Office: U.S. DEPARTMENT OF COMMERCE
Under the Paperwork Reduction Act of 1995, no persons are required to respond to a collection of information unless it displays a valid OMB control number.

# TRANSMITTAL FORM

*(to be used for all correspondence after initial filing)*

| | |
|---|---|
| **Application Number** | |
| **Filing Date** | |
| **First Named Inventor** | |
| Group Art Unit | |
| Examiner Name | |
| Total Number of Pages in This Submission | Attorney Docket Number |

## ENCLOSURES (check all that apply)

☐ Fee Transmittal Form

☐ Fee Attached

☐ Amendment / Response

☐ After Final

☐ Extension of Time Request

☐ Express Abandonment Request

☐ Information Disclosure Statement

☐ Certified Copy of Priority Document(s)

☐ Response to Missing Parts/ Incomplete Application

☐ Response to Missing Parts under 37 CFR 1.52 or 1.53

☐ Assignment Papers *(for an Application)*

☐ Drawing(s)

☐ Licensing-related Papers

☐ Petition Checklist and Accompanying Petition

☐ To Convert a Provisional Application

☐ Power of Attorney, Revocation Change of Correspondence Address

☐ Terminal Disclaimer

☐ After Allowance Communication to Group

☐ Appeal Communication to Board of Appeals and Interferences

☐ Appeal Communication to Group *(Appeal Notice, Brief, Reply Brief)*

☐ Proprietary Information

☐ Status Letter

☐ Additional Enclosure(s) *(please identify below):*

Remarks

### SIGNATURE OF APPLICANT, ATTORNEY, OR AGENT

| Firm *or* Individual name | |
|---|---|
| Signature | |
| Date | |

### CERTIFICATE OF MAILING

I hereby certify that this correspondence is being deposited with the United States Postal Service as first class mail in an envelope addressed to: Assistant Commissioner for Patents, Washington, D.C. 20231 on this date:

| Typed or printed name | |
|---|---|
| Signature | Date |

## REQUEST FOR EXTENSION OF TIME

IN THE UNITED STATES PATENT AND TRADEMARK OFFICE

| | |
|---|---|
| Applicant: | Examiner: |
| Serial No.: | Group Art Unit: |
| Filed: | |
| Title: | |

REQUEST FOR EXTENSION OF TIME

Honorable Commissioner of Patents and Trademarks
Washington, D.C. 20231

Sir:

An Office Action dated_____, was mailed in the above referenced patent application setting a due date for a response of_____. Applicant(s) hereby request(s) a _____-month extension of time to and including the date of_____in which to file the required response. Enclosed is a check in the amount of $_____ for payment of the fees for said extension.

Respectfully submitted,

Date:

Direct Communications To:

## AMENDMENT AND RESPONSE

IN THE UNITED STATES PATENT AND TRADEMARK OFFICE

Applicant:                          Examiner:
Serial No.:                         Group Art Unit:
Filed:
Title:

AMENDMENT AND RESPONSE

Honorable Commissioner of Patents and Trademarks
Washington, D.C. 20231

Sir:

This Amendment and Response is submitted in response to the Examiner's Office Action dated _____. Please amend the above identified application as follows:

In the specification:

In the claims:

REMARKS

Reconsideration of the application as amended is respectfully requested.

Respectfully submitted,

Date:

Direct Communications To:

## NOTICE OF APPEAL

IN THE UNITED STATES PATENT AND TRADEMARK OFFICE

Applicant:                                      Examiner:
Serial No.:                                     Group Art Unit:
Filed:
For:

NOTICE OF APPEAL

Honorable Commissioner of Patents and Trademarks
Box AF
Washington, D.C. 20231

Sir:

In reply to the Office Action, mailed_____, Applicant(s) hereby appeal(s) to the Board of Appeals and Interferences from the decision of the Primary Examiner finally rejecting claims_____ in the above identified application. In accordance with 37 C.F.R. § 1.17(e), enclosed is the fee for filing a Notice of Appeal in the amount of $_____.

Respectfully submitted,


Date:


Direct Communications To:

Use this Certificate of Mailing when the correspondences indicated below are filed by First-Class Mail:

## CERTIFICATE OF MAILING PURSUANT TO 37 C.F.R. SECTION 1.8

I hereby certify that this correspondence as indicated below:

☐ Request for Extension of Time
☐ Amendment and Response
☐ Notice of Appeal
☐ Other _____

is being deposited with the United States Postal Service as First-Class Mail in an envelope addressed to Commissioner of Patents and Trademarks, Washington, D.C. 20231 on

_____

DATE OF DEPOSIT

_____

NAME OF APPLICANT OR REGISTERED REPRESENTATIVE

_____

SIGNATURE

# Infringement of Patents

A NEW U.S. PATENT grants for a term of twenty years from the date on which the application for patent was filed "the right to exclude others from making, using, offering for sale, or selling the invention throughout the United States or importing the invention into the United States." Under the recently enacted General Agreement on Tariffs and Trade (GATT) legislation, the term of a U.S. patent was changed from seventeen years from its issuance to twenty years from its U.S. filing date. If the invention is a process, the statute now grants the right to exclude others from making, using, offering for sale, or selling throughout the United States or importing into the United States products made by the patented process. Any violation of these federal rights constitute patent infringement. If a patent is infringed, the patentee may sue for relief in the appropriate federal court. The patentee may ask the court for an injunction to prevent the continuation of the infringement and may also ask the court for an award of damages because of the infringement. In such an infringement suit, the defendant may raise the question of the validity of the patent, which is then decided by the court. The defendant may also aver that what is being done does not constitute infringement.

An understanding of which acts constitute patent infringement is important in determining the protection a patent provides for your invention. Naturally, once your patent issues, you should ensure that you are cognizant of others who may be infringing. Keep in mind that your patent is not self-enforcing and you have to monitor the market for infringing activities and take action to stop them.

## The Categories of Patent Infringement

The specific acts that constitute patent infringement are defined by statute (subsections (a) through (g) of 35 U.S.C. § 271) and may be through the "direct" actions of an infringer or through actions which cause another to infringe (i.e., contributory or inducement of infringement).

Direct infringement occurs when, without authority, the infringer makes, uses, offers to sell, or sells any patented invention within the United States or imports into the United States any patented invention during the term of the patent. Infringement occurs even if only one of the proscribed activities is performed. But, one of the prohibited acts must actually occur—the mere threat of future activities does not constitute infringement. Direct infringement occurs when the infringer has made an operable embodiment of the patented invention.

Certain activities, which may appear to be infringements, are permitted. For example, it is not an infringement if someone makes or uses a patented invention solely for experimental purposes that do not advance any significant business interest. This so-called experimental use exception is a narrow one. If someone manufactures or uses the patented invention for experimental tests in preparation for commercial exploitation, this is considered an infringement.

In addition, if a patented product is purchased from the patentee, or one with authority to sell the patented product (e.g., a licensee of the patent owner), the purchaser may use and resell that product in the United States free of any risk of infringement. The purchaser may also make repairs on the patented product and replace worn out parts, but he or she cannot completely reconstruct an entirely new product when the original product, viewed as a whole, has become spent. Although the rule is straightforward, its application is less so because it is not always clear how much repair is allowed before an item is deemed to be reconstructed.

Liability for patent infringement due to indirect infringement applies to those who actively induce or contribute to the infringement of a patent. Active inducement is often described as aiding and abetting another's direct infringement. Contributory infringement is the selling of a component, material, or apparatus that constitutes a material part of a patented invention, where the seller knows that the component, material, or apparatus is "especially made or especially adapted for use in an infringement of such patent, and not a staple article or commodity of commerce suitable for substantial noninfringing use."

A wide range of actions may be found to induce or contribute to another's infringement. To prove inducement of infringement, you need to show that the infringer knew or should have known that his or her actions would cause infringement by another. To prove contributory infringement, you need only show that the infringer sold a material part of a patented invention with knowledge that such part is especially made or adapted for infringement and has no substantial noninfringing use. Protection against inducement of infringement and contributory infringement may be very important for the owners of method patents, because it is usually impractical to sue the large numbers of individual purchasers who are using products to practice the patented method. Nevertheless, both active inducement and contributory infringement are predicated on direct infringement of the patent at issue for, without such direct infringement, there can be neither contributory infringement nor inducement of infringement.

## General Principles of an Infringement Analysis

If you believe that another is infringing your patent, you should first find out as much as possible about the infringing process or product. Once you have gathered this information, use the following guideline to assess whether the product or process actually infringes the claims of your patent.

It is important to note that, although a patent may comprise a description, examples, drawings, an abstract, and claims, only the claims of a patent can be infringed. To determine whether a product or process infringes, you must, therefore, compare the allegedly infringing product or process to your patent claims. This is ordinarily done in two separate steps. The first step is to construe or interpret the scope of the claims: What do the claims, as they are written, actually cover? The second step is to compare the properly construed claims with the accused composition, device, or method to determine whether it contains all the elements recited in the claims and therefore infringes the patent claims. If the accused composition, device, or method meets all the limitations of a claim, it infringes. Although many patents contain more than one claim, if the accused composition, device, or process infringes only a single claim, it still infringes the patent.

In determining the meanings of the words of a patent claim to construe or interpret its scope, first consider the language of the claim itself. A determination of what a patent claim actually covers is often complex and rarely is uncontroverted. For example, the language of the claim must be construed in light of the other claims, the specification, the prior art, and the prosecution history of the patent. Express representations to the patent examiner regarding the meanings of the terms used in the claim will also affect the claim scope.

Claims are construed as they would be by persons skilled in the relevant art, but a patent applicant can define his or her terms as he or she so chooses—even in a manner contrary to their ordinary meanings. Words must, of course, be used consistently in both the claims and the specification. Further, the terms of a claim will be given their ordinary meaning, unless it appears that the inventor used them differently.

Claims are generally not limited to any specific or preferred embodiment or example disclosed in the patent. Accordingly, it is improper to read a limitation from the patent specification into a claim, unless the limitation is actually required. It is, however, entirely proper to consult the patent specification to determine the correct meaning of a claim term that is in dispute.

It is presumed that two claims which differ in wording have

different meanings and scopes; this is known as the "doctrine of claim differentiation." Under this settled rule, specific limitations set forth in narrow claims cannot be read into broader claims. Moreover, a claim must be given the same meaning for purposes of both validity and infringement analyses. In areas of complex technology, an evaluation of how a court may construe patent claims may require an in-depth analysis by an experienced patent attorney.

After the claims have been properly construed, they are compared with the suspected infringing composition, device, or process. Literal infringement requires that every limitation of the claim must be literally present in the accused device. For example, if an invention claims a computer system comprising a modem, monitor, and keyboard, it would not be infringed by a system containing only a monitor and a keyboard, but no modem. The infringement analysis is rarely this simple, as it is complicated by the manner in which the claims are written and the legal concepts applied to determine infringement.

For example, an element in a claim may be expressed as a means or step for performing a specified function without the recital of structure. So-called means-plus-function claims are an exception to the general rule regarding literal infringement as those claims literally cover, not only the relevant structure, material, or acts described in the specification to perform the specified function, but also their equivalents. Therefore, certain products may be found to literally infringe means-plus-function claims even though they contain components not specifically claimed.

## Infringement Under the Doctrine of Equivalents

Even though you may conclude that a device or process is not within the literal scope of a patent claim, it may, under certain circumstances, infringe under the "doctrine of equivalents." This doctrine was created to extend liability to infringers who misappropriate the benefits of an invention while avoiding the literal language of patent claims. The U.S. Supreme Court has recognized that to permit infringers to subordinate substance to form and, thereby deprive inventors of the full benefits of their inventions, would discourage the disclosure of inventions through patents, and thereby frustrate one of the primary purposes of the patent system.

Thus, an accused product, although outside the literal scope of the claim, may still infringe under the doctrine of equivalents if that product substantially performs the same function in the same way to obtain the same overall result as the claimed invention. This three-pronged test (i.e., function/way/result) is applied to the claimed invention as a whole, not to the individual limitations of the claim. Still, the rule further requires that all claim limitations, or their substantial equivalents, must be found in the accused device. Thus, the doctrine of equivalents does not really expand the scope of the patent claims, but, rather, the doctrine expands the right to exclude to equivalents of what is claimed.

The courts have not articulated any specific test that must be followed to show that a substitute for a claim limitation in the accused product is the substantial equivalent of the limitation recited in the claim. Thus, the function/way/result analysis is an acceptable way, but not the only way, to show equivalence. A determination of equivalency is made in view of the patent, the state of the relevant technology at the time the invention in question was made (i.e., the prior art), and the particular facts of a given case.

The purpose and function of a particular element and the qualities it has when combined with other elements are proper considerations when determining infringement under the doctrine of equivalents. An important factor is whether those reasonably skilled in the art would know that the accused element is interchangeable with the limitation in the patent claim. Proof of equivalence can be made in many forms such as expert testimony, treatises, disclosures in the prior art, and technological demonstrations and tests. While a substantial equivalent for each claim limitation must be found in the accused product, a one-to-one correspondence between the claim limitations and the elements of the accused product is not necessary under the doctrine of equivalents. Other factors being equal, a pioneering invention is entitled to a broad range of equivalents and a modest advance in a crowded art is only entitled to a narrow range of equivalents.

The doctrine of equivalents serves important public policies by encouraging the disclosure of inventions in patents and protecting research and development investments. But, when the reach of a patent is extended too far under this doctrine, two different public policies are frustrated. First, the public has the right to fair notice of where the boundaries of a claimed invention lie so that others can avoid infringing the patent. Second, the important policy of encouraging others to advance technology by successfully designing around patents is frustrated when the boundaries of a patent claim cannot be determined or are drawn too broadly under the doctrine of equivalents. In recognition of these polices, the doctrine of equivalents cannot be used to ensnare an accused device already disclosed in the prior art and cannot be used to recapture claim coverage clearly given up during prosecution before the PTO.

The converse principle to the doctrine of equivalents is the "reverse doctrine of equivalents." The reverse doctrine of equivalents provides that an accused product or process does not infringe, even though it is covered by the literal language of a patent claim, if the product or process has been so drastically changed in principle that it performs the same or similar function in a substantially different way. Put another way, this doctrine prevents a finding of infringement when the accused device is so dissimilar to those contemplated by the inventor that it would be inequitable to regard the accused device as being within the scope of the patent claims. The reverse doctrine of equivalents has been successfully employed to avert a finding of literal infringement, although only on rare occasions.

## Taking Action Against Infringement

Once you have determined that your patent is being infringed, contact an experienced patent attorney to pursue appropriate action against the infringement. Although it is not required that you obtain legal representation to enforce your patent, it is very difficult and surely unwise for one who is not lawyer to handle the complexities of patent litigation. Patent litigation is expensive, and the legal fees to enforce a patent through litigation will, in even what may appear to be the simplest of cases, likely exceed $500,000. Some patent attorneys, although clearly not the majority, will handle patent infringement cases on a contingent fee basis.

Legal action for patent infringement is brought in the appropriate U.S. district court. An action for infringement of a patent must be filed within six years of occurrence of the infringing activity. The patent owner can recover damages from the infringer as well as an injunction to stop future infringing activities.

Suits for infringement of patents follow the rules of procedure of the federal courts. From the decision of the district court, there is an appeal to the Court of Appeals for the Federal Circuit. The U.S. Supreme Court may thereafter take a case by writ of certiorari. If the U.S. government infringes a patent, the patentee has a remedy for damages in the U.S. claims court. The government may use any patented invention without permission of the patentee, but the patentee is entitled to obtain compensation for the use by or for the government.

Fortunately, you may be able to enforce your patent and obtain compensation for its infringement without a lawsuit. Usually, the first step is to contact the infringer. Depending on your objectives, you can offer the infringer a license under the patent or some other business arrangement wherein you allow him or her to sell the accused product. However, you should consider, before sending a cease and desist letter, that if you charge someone with infringement, he or she may sue you to obtain a declaration that the patent was invalid or was not infringed. As a result of your threat of enforcement, you can be unwittingly brought into an expensive litigation.

## What If Your Activities Infringe a Patent

If you intend to make, sell, or import a new product or process, determine whether your intended activity is patented by someone else. Even though you can never be certain that what you intend to do is free from the patent protection of another party, you can minimize your risks by doing a little research.

There are private companies that, for a relatively inexpensive fee, will search the patent literature for patents that may relate to your product or process. Alternatively, you can, on your own, obtain information about whether products similar to yours are protected by patents through product literature (which often contains patent information) or the product itself (which is often marked with a patent number). Naturally, if you are copying the product or process of another, you should carefully assess whether it is patented. If you identify patents that are in force and may cover your product or process, obtain copies of the patents from the PTO and perform the infringement analysis described above. Where questions of possible infringement arise and you still desire to proceed with the sale of the composition, device, or process, you should obtain competent legal advice so the risks of infringement, which can be substantial, are properly evaluated.

Be aware that the patent statute authorizes the court to award up to three times the amount of the actual damages caused by the infringement and to award attorney fees where the case is found to be "exceptional." When the court finds that infringement has been willful, exceptional circumstances may be found to exist and enhanced damages may be properly granted. It is, therefore, paramount that when you face an issue of infringement, you avoid a finding that your infringement has been willful.

Simply stated, your infringement will be found to have been willful if you acted in disregard for the patent. Your infringement is willful if you have no reasonable basis for believing you were not infringing.

You must have had actual notice of the patent to be found guilty of willful infringement. There is a duty, from the time you become aware of a patent, to either cease the allegedly infringing activity or form a good faith belief of patent invalidity or noninfringement.

Willfulness is determined by the totality of the circumstances. Generally, infringement will not be found to have been willful if (1) you possess a good faith belief that the patent is invalid or the allegedly infringing device does not infringe, (2) you had reason to believe that the infringing act was covered by a license, or (3) you made a good faith attempt to alter the device or process to avoid infringement.

Although the presence or absence of a legal opinion is not necessarily determinative, the courts have often relied solely on the quality of a legal opinion to determine whether or not the infringement was willful. A comprehensive legal opinion will generally be considered by the court as strong evidence of a good faith belief that the infringing activity was permitted.

Questions of patent infringement are almost always complex and are rarely amenable to simple resolution. When faced with a question as to whether your activities may infringe a patent, or whether another is infringing a patent that you own, it is almost always prudent to consult an experienced patent attorney.

Naturally, if your attorneys conclude that your activities will infringe a valid patent, you may attempt to seek a license under the patent. Obviously, seeking a license will bring your possible infringing activities to the attention of the patent owner. Moreover, a patent owner is under no obligation to grant you a license under his or her invention (See chapter 12 for a review of licensing).

## Patent Marking

A patentee who makes or sells patented articles, or a person who does so for the patentee, is required to mark the articles with the word "patent" and the number of the patent. If the articles are not marked, the patentee may not recover damages from an infringer unless the infringer was duly notified of the infringement and continued to infringe after the notice.

It is against the law to mark an article as patented when it is not, and the offender is subject to penalty.

Some persons mark articles sold with the terms "patent applied for" or "patent pending." These phrases have no legal effect, and only state that an application for patent has been filed in the PTO. The protection afforded by a patent does not start until the actual grant of the patent. False use of these phrases, or their equivalent, is prohibited.

# CHAPTER 11

# Foreign Patent Rights

ONCE YOU HAVE FILED a patent application in the United States, consider whether or not you as the inventor (or the assignee if the invention has been assigned to some other entity) wish to pursue patent protection for the invention in countries other than the United States. Keep in mind that the rights and privileges afforded by your U.S. patent gives you the ability to prevent others from using, making, or selling your invention in the United States as defined by the claims in your patent. If similar applications are not filed in other countries, there is nothing to prevent someone in a foreign jurisdiction from copying your invention and making, using, or selling it.

This chapter will provide a review of the basic rules and requirements for filing a foreign patent application when you have a properly filed U.S. patent application covering an invention. Patent laws and regulations vary among countries and the specific requirements of each is not covered in this book.

## Filing Your Patent Abroad

United States patents provide protection only within the boundaries of the United States and its territories—they have no effect on activities outside the Unites States. An exception, however, are process patents, which can enable you to prevent the importation of infringing goods made overseas using the patented process. Also, a U.S. patent might be influential in getting corresponding patents allowed in some foreign countries. For all practical purposes, however, a U.S. patent protects only the market in the United States against infringing products.

Patent protection is granted on a country-by-country basis. It is therefore necessary to obtain a patent in each country where the inventor wants the right to stop others from making, using, or selling the invention.

Every inventor probably would like to patent his or her invention around the world and gain as extensive a monopoly as possible for the invention. A major factor to consider, however, is that obtaining patents in foreign countries is generally very expensive. Because of the expense, and other important issues, the countries in which a patent will be pursued should be carefully selected. An inventor, before applying for foreign patents, should be satisfied that he or she could make some profit or satisfy some particular reason for obtaining them.

Expenses, such as legal fees, translation costs, filing fees, and periodic maintenance fees, must be taken into account when deciding where to file foreign patent applications. Select countries where a significant market exists for your invention and where there are realistic manufacturing, marketing, or licensing opportunities for you. Avoid countries that have weak patent laws or difficult procedures for enforcing patents against infringers.

Remember that the patent laws of many countries differ from those of the United States. Publication of the invention before the date of filing the patent application will bar the right to a patent in most foreign countries. Maintenance fees are required in most foreign countries. Many countries require that the patented invention be manufactured in that country within a certain period, usually three years. The patent can be void in some countries if there is no manufacture within this period, although in most countries the patent can be subject to the grant of compulsory licenses to any person who may apply for a license.

After you have decided to seek foreign patent protection and have selected the countries of interest, file a national patent application in each country or file a central Patent Cooperation Treaty (PCT) application or European patent application. The foreign application is usually filed in a central clearing house, such as the European Patent Office (EPO) or in the PTO, under the PCT. Filing with the EPO or PCT, the applicant designates the countries in which patent protection is sought. The EPO and PCT applications are first examined and prosecuted in a central filing office. The applications subsequently enter what is called "the national phase" where they are filed in each of the designated countries.

. As already discussed, this process can cost a considerable amount of money. For example, there are filing fees for the initial filing of the application in the PCT receiving office or the EPO, and legal fees will certainly be incurred during the prosecution of the application. Once the application enters the national phase, additional application fees are required for each respective country, and translations may also be required if the country is non-English speaking. A foreign patent agent or attorney will likely be hired in each country to handle most of the paperwork and ensure all the local rules are followed and that the formal papers are properly executed and filed. Miscellaneous filing fees are often incurred and maintenance fees are required in most countries after the patent issues in order to keep it valid and enforceable.

Before incurring the costs of filing patent applications in foreign countries, determine whether or not the invention will be manufactured or sold outside the United States, and, if so, the likelihood of its commercial success. It is not worth going through the effort and expense of filing a patent application in a foreign country unless the invention will likely be of substantial commercial value in that country. When considering the commercial value of your invention, determine whether it will be marketed and/or sold by you or your affiliate, or whether it will have licensing potential in the foreign countries. Keep in mind that, although you may not have the ability or the desire to manufacture, market, or sell your invention overseas, others may be interested in doing so if the invention is likely to become a commercial success.

If foreign patent rights are obtained, others who wish to practice your invention in the respective countries will have to take a license under the foreign patents, which can generate royalty income for you. Foreign patents can also be beneficial if someone wants to obtain a license to make and sell your patented invention here in the United States as well as abroad.

You must obtain a foreign filing license from the PTO before you file a foreign patent application or otherwise transmit information concerning your invention abroad. You can request a foreign filing license from the PTO, but one is routinely granted within six months of filing a U.S. patent application. You can proceed with foreign filing even if you have not received a foreign filing license if six months or more have passed since filing your U.S. patent application.

Remember that to protect your ability to obtain foreign patents, it is important to make sure your invention is not publicly disclosed prior to filing the foreign patent application. As discussed earlier, any publication, sale, or public disclosure of the invention in any form prior to filing an application is an automatic bar to patentability in most foreign countries. Only in the United States and a few foreign countries, such as Canada, is there a grace period from the date of such disclosure to when the application must be filed in order to preserve the right to a patent.

Even if you are able to handle filing and prosecuting your U.S. patent application, seek the advice of foreign patent attorneys or agents to ensure all necessary requirements are met when filing in another country. Foreign patent attorneys and agents in various countries are listed in the *Martindale-Hubbell Law Directory*, which is available at most libraries. Foreign patent attorneys and agents can also be found through organizations such as the American Intellectual Property Law Association. Additionally, there are attorneys and law firms in the United States that specialize in filing and prosecuting patent applications abroad.

There are several important treaties and international rules governing patents and patent applications. These treaties and rules have been adopted by most industrial countries in an attempt to harmonize the various patent systems around the world. One of the earliest treaties is the International Convention for the Protection of Industrial Property entered into in Paris in 1883 (referred to as the Paris Convention). The Paris Convention allows a patent applicant to claim the benefit of the earlier filing date of the first-filed patent application for foreign applications filed within one year thereof. The European Patent Convention forms a central EPO where a single patent application can be filed that covers most of Europe. Another important treaty is the PCT under which a single patent application can be filed designating nearly eighty countries.

A list of the countries and their memberships in the various patent treaties is provided at the end of this chapter.

## Earlier Filing Dates Under the Paris Convention

The most important aspect of the Paris Convention is that any application initially filed within one member country may be filed in any other member country within one year, and the patent application in the other country will receive the same earlier filing date as the first-filed application. For example, if you file a patent application for your new invention on January 1, 1997, in a Paris Convention country, you have until December 31, 1997, to file in any other member country under the treaty. Hence, prior art or acts between the first patent filing and the later foreign filings that might otherwise present a bar or obstacle to patentability will have no effect under the Paris Convention because the later foreign-filed applications are given the earlier effective filing date. This allows an inventor to file a patent application in one country, such as the United States, and delay other filings for nearly one year while the invention is being marketed or evaluated. You can still file a foreign patent application after the one-year period has passed under the Paris Convention, but the filing date of these applications will be the actual date the application is filed in each respective country. These applications could become granted patents provided no sale or publication of the invention has taken place that would destroy patentability.

As mentioned earlier, the one-year grace period for filing abroad is quite beneficial because once the first patent application has been filed, the inventor can market or otherwise exploit his invention and get an idea of the commercial potential of the invention. If the invention enjoys considerable success from the beginning, the inventor may want to file in more countries to get greater control of the worldwide market. On the other hand, if the invention is a relative flop during the year preceding foreign filing, the applicant may find it prudent to file in just a few countries, if any at all, and thereby save considerable time and money.

## The European Patent Office

The countries from the European Economic Community entered into an agreement in 1978 known as the European Patent Convention that establishes a central filing depository for filing a patent application. This depository is known as the EPO and is located in Munich, Germany. Filing a patent application in the EPO is tantamount to filing in all the specific enumerated countries that are members of the European Patent Convention. The EPO examines the patent application for all the selected countries, and once the patent is issued, it can be registered for granting in each of the selected member countries.

Any application filed in the EPO that is based on a previously filed U.S. counterpart application can receive the earlier filing date with the PTO provided the application is filed within one year from the U.S. filing date. If this European application matures into a European patent, it can issue as a patent in each of the designated countries and these national patents will have the same effective filing date as the U.S. parent patent application.

The prosecution of a European patent application differs in many respects from prosecuting a patent application in the United States. All patent applications filed in the PTO are subjected to an ex parte examination (the only parties involved are the applicant and the patent examiner), which is carried out in secrecy. However, in the EPO, all applications are published six months after they have been filed in the office. This publication is essentially an invitation to the world to comment on the patentability of the invention described therein. While the patent examiner in the EPO conducts his or her own prior art search, the published application may cause someone to submit any relevant prior art or to prepare to file an opposition to the grant of a European patent.

Filing a patent application in the EPO offers several advantages, such as the ability to file and prosecute the application in English, a single prosecution that includes all the EPO countries, a thorough examination of the application, reduced costs where patents will be pursued in a large number of countries, and a quicker grant issuance of relatively strong patents. Some disadvantages are increased costs in filing in only a small number of countries, a fairly rigid application format, and a possible loss of essentially all European patent rights if the European patent application is rejected or successfully opposed.

If a European patent is granted, it issues in each of the respective designated countries and will be effective for twenty years from the date of filing. Keep in mind that maintenance fees must be paid in each of these countries during the life of the patent and in the EPO during prosecution.

## The Patent Cooperation Treaty

Filing a patent application under the PCT is rapidly becoming the most popular and cost-effective method for filing abroad. The PCT provides a centralized filing and searching system for a single international patent application. The PCT application process is intended to simplify filing a patent application in foreign countries, eliminate the need to duplicate patent filing and searching, and reduce the costs of filing for patents around the world.

Filing through the PCT involves filing a PCT patent application in any member country, such as the United States, and designating the countries where the filing is to be effective. Separate translated national applications must be filed in each country of interest under the PCT within the required time after the filing date of the PCT application.

For a U.S. inventor, the PCT application is typically filed in the United States either initially as a PCT application or within one year of, and claiming the benefit of, an earlier regular or provisional U.S. patent application. Generally, eight months after the filing date of the PCT application or twenty months after the filing date of the initial U.S. patent application, the national filings of the PCT application is made in each designated country. If an election to proceed under Chapter II of the PCT is made before nineteen months after filing an initial U.S. patent application, the separate national filings can be delayed for thirty months after the U.S. filing date.

Hence, under the PCT, a U.S. patent applicant can take either twenty or thirty months from the original filing date of the U.S. patent application to decide where to file abroad. This grace period can be extremely beneficial in that it gives the applicant a considerable amount of time to determine to what degree his or her invention is a commercial success in the United States and to what scope of claim coverage can be expected from the U.S. patent once it is granted. This insight can be of great benefit in deciding the likelihood of patent protection in the other countries as well as the extent of foreign filings and the cost versus benefit therefrom.

There are important advantages in filing a patent application under the PCT. As mentioned already, the PCT application allows time to evaluate the commercial potential and patentability of the invention before having to make a final decision on foreign filing. Other advantages are that the payment of national fees and translation costs are postponed, foreign applications under the PCT can be filed later than those not filed via PCT, and a stronger patent may be issued in some countries. The disadvantages of filing a PCT application are the relatively complex procedures, additional paperwork, and longer delays in obtaining a patent.

Remember that an inventor can always file for foreign patents without following the procedures of the PCT, EPO, or Paris Convention. Instead, the inventor would file a nonconvention national application in each country of interest. Be sure to obtain a foreign filing license from the PTO or wait until six months or more after the U.S. filing date of your application before filing any patent application outside the United States, or you will lose your right to obtain a U.S. patent.

## The Effect of the General Agreement on Tariffs and Trade on Patents

The General Agreement onf Tariffs and Trade (GATT) was entered into by most industrialized countries and has had a major impact on patents. Any in-depth discussion of the ramifications of GATT would require far more space than is available in this book because the agreement is extensive and covers more than intellectual property issues. The important thing to remember is that the GATT agreement went a long way in harmonizing the patent laws of the United States with those of most other countries of the world.

Prior to June 7, 1995, for example, the term of a patent in the United States was seventeen years from the date the patent issued. Patent terms in most industrialized countries lasted twenty years from the earliest filing date of the patent application. Under GATT, now in the United States for applications filed before June 7, 1995, the term is either seventeen years from the date of issue or twenty years from the earliest filing date, whichever is longer. The patent term for U.S. patent applications filed on or after June 7, 1995, is twenty years from the earliest filing date in the United States.

General Agreement on Tariffs and Trade has also changed the nature of interference contests where priority of inventorship is determined when two or more inventors are applying for a patent on the same invention in the United States. Priority of invention in the United States is determined by who was first to invent. Evidence of activities outside the United States, which had been previously excluded, can now be used to show dates of invention in interference proceedings. Unlike the United States, most countries award priority of invention to the inventor who was the first to file. It is debatable whether GATT will influence the United States to adopt the first-to-file system used by most countries.

## List of Countries and Memberships in Patent Treaties

| COUNTRY | PARIS | EPO | PCT | COUNTRY | PARIS | EPO | PCT |
|---|---|---|---|---|---|---|---|
| Algeria | Y | N | N | India | N | N | N |
| Argentina | Y | N | N | Indonesia | Y | N | N |
| Armenia | Y | N | Y | Iran | N | N | N |
| Australia | Y | N | Y | Iraq | Y | N | N |
| Austria | Y | Y | Y | Ireland | Y | N | Y |
| Barbados | Y | N | Y | Israel | Y | N | N |
| Belarus | Y | N | Y | Italy | Y | Y | Y |
| Belgium | Y | Y | Y | Jamaica | N | N | N |
| Brazil | Y | N | Y | Japan | Y | N | Y |
| Bulgaria | Y | N | Y | Jordan | Y | N | N |
| Canada | Y | N | Y | Kazakhstan | Y | N | Y |
| Chile | N | N | N | Kenya | Y | N | N |
| China | Y | N | Y | Kuwait | N | N | N |
| Columbia | N | N | N | Kyrgyzstan | Y | N | Y |
| Costa Rica | N | N | N | Latvia | Y | N | Y |
| Cuba | Y | N | N | Liberia | Y | N | Y |
| Czech Republic | Y | N | Y | Libya | Y | N | N |
| Denmark | Y | Y | Y | Liechtenstein | Y | Y | Y |
| Ecuador | N | N | N | Lithuania | Y | N | Y |
| Egypt | Y | N | N | Luxembourg | Y | Y | Y |
| El Salvador | N | N | N | Madagascar | Y | N | Y |
| Estonia | Y | N | Y | Malawi | Y | N | Y |
| Ethiopia | N | N | N | Malaysia | N | N | N |
| Finland | Y | N | Y | Mexico | Y | N | Y |
| France | Y | Y | Y | Moldavia | Y | N | Y |
| Gambia | N | N | N | Moldoro | Y | N | Y |
| Georgia | Y | N | Y | Monaco | Y | N | Y |
| Germany | Y | Y | Y | Mongolia | Y | N | Y |
| Ghana | Y | N | N | Morocco | Y | N | N |
| Greece | Y | Y | Y | Netherlands | Y | Y | Y |
| Guatemala | N | N | N | New Zealand | Y | N | Y |
| Honduras | N | N | N | Nicaragua | N | N | N |
| Hong Kong | N | N | N | Niger | Y | N | Y |
| Hungary | Y | N | Y | North Korea | Y | N | Y |
| Iceland | Y | N | Y | Norway | Y | N | Y |

| COUNTRY | PARIS | EPO | PCT | COUNTRY | PARIS | EPO | PCT |
|---|---|---|---|---|---|---|---|
| Pakistan | N | N | N | Yugoslavia | Y | N | N |
| Panama | N | N | N | Zaire | Y | N | N |
| Paraguay | N | N | N | Zimbabwe | Y | N | N |
| Peru | N | N | N | | | | |
| Philippines | Y | N | N | | | | |
| Poland | Y | N | Y | | | | |
| Portugal | Y | N | Y | | | | |
| Romania | Y | N | Y | | | | |
| Russian Federation | Y | N | Y | | | | |
| Sierra Leone | N | N | N | | | | |
| Singapore | Y | N | Y | | | | |
| Slovak Republic | Y | N | Y | | | | |
| Slovenia | Y | N | Y | | | | |
| South Africa | Y | N | N | | | | |
| South Korea | Y | N | Y | | | | |
| Spain | Y | Y | Y | | | | |
| Sri Lanka | Y | N | Y | | | | |
| Sudan | Y | N | Y | | | | |
| Swaziland | Y | N | Y | | | | |
| Sweden | Y | Y | Y | | | | |
| Switzerland | Y | Y | Y | | | | |
| Syria | Y | N | N | | | | |
| Taiwan | N | N | N | | | | |
| Tajikistan | Y | N | Y | | | | |
| Thailand | N | N | N | | | | |
| Trinidad & Tobago | Y | N | Y | | | | |
| Turkey | Y | N | N | | | | |
| Turkmenistan | Y | N | Y | | | | |
| Uganda | Y | N | Y | | | | |
| Ukraine | Y | N | Y | | | | |
| United Kingdom | Y | Y | Y | | | | |
| United States | Y | N | Y | | | | |
| Uzbekistan | Y | N | Y | | | | |
| Venezuela | N | N | N | | | | |
| Vietnam | Y | N | Y | | | | |

# Licensing Your Patents and Inventions

A S EXPLAINED EARLIER, intellectual property—patents, trademarks, and copyrights—can be bought, sold, and exploited like other forms of personal and real property. For this reason, the exploitation of intellectual property, in particular patents, has become a significant element of the financial strategy of small and large businesses as well as opportunities for individual inventors to derive economic benefit from their inventions.

## Understanding the Value of Licensing

Licensing is a form of intellectual property exploitation that allows an inventor or owner of the invention to capitalize on the financial earning power of patents, trademarks, and copyrights by making them available for use in exchange for some level of consideration. Licensing allows a patent owner to exploit the value of the patent without giving up ownership and control of the patent or having to work to bring the patent to commercialization. The owner, or licensor, generally collects lump-sum payments and/or running royalties without assuming any business risks.

The process of licensing begins with the inventor's or owner's understanding and evaluation of the intrinsic value of the patent or invention. This involves examining a number of factors to determine how much the patent and invention is worth and how to maximize the value. Does the invention represent a technological break-through? Has the invention been fully developed or commercialized? What are the real or perceived benefits of the invention? Is the invention adequately protected by patents or other intellectual property rights? These are some of the questions you must answer before you can determine the licensing potential of your invention.

You should realize that an invention not protected by a patent will likely have little or no licensing potential. No one wants to pay for a license to an invention that the rest of the world can practice freely. Likewise, prospective licensees may not have a strong interest in an invention that has limited marketability.

It is important that the inventor or patent owner size up the market in which the respective patent or invention would compete. As explained in chapter 1, you will need to assess the commercial potential and marketability of your invention before you can begin to measure its licensing value. This may require market studies and an analysis of your invention in comparison to similar products as well as unrelated alternatives. Look at other licensing agreements that you may have access to for determining customary royalties and conditions. When this analysis is complete, you are ready to examine licensing as a way to exploit your intellectual property. You may want to seek the assistance of a patent attorney or invention broker in preparing for and going through the licensing process.

## Licensing Requirements and Considerations

If someone else wants to legally make, use, sell, or import your patented invention, he or she would need a license from you. A license used in connection with patents essentially provides assurances that the person or entity practicing the patented invention will not be sued by the patent owner for infringement. In exchange for receiving a license, the licensee pays a royalty or lump sum or both to the patent owner as the licensor.

A patent license is basically a contract and requires the essential elements of an offer, acceptance, and consideration. The license is a negotiated agreement that should always be in writing and signed by both the licensee and licensor.

The license agreement can be simple or complex depending on the terms and conditions required by the parties. A sample license agreement is provided at the end of this chapter; this form can be used for most simple patent licensing situations. Keep in mind, however, that each licensing agreement is a distinct transaction with terms that are negotiated and agreed to by the parties on a case-by-case basis.

There are several fundamental prerequisites to creating an effective patent license. First, the party granting the license must have ownership of the patent. Second, the license must specify what rights are being granted. The license should also indicate the consideration (e.g., royalties or lump-sum payments) that is being paid by the licensee to the patent owner. The patent license must also be free of instances of patent misuse and antitrust violations.

The ownership of an invention and any patent covering it originally lies with the inventor. The inventor can then assign his or her ownership of the invention and patent to another party or retain ownership and license the patent to another party. If the inventor retains ownership of the patent, nothing more is required to evidence this ownership because the patent itself will issue in the inventor's name. If the inventor transfers ownership, then a written patent assignment should be executed by the inventor and recorded with the PTO.

If the inventor decides to license rather than assign the patented invention, a written license agreement is needed. The license agreement should be executed by both the inventor, as patent owner, and the licensee. Patent licenses usually are not filed for recording with the PTO.

The licensor grants permission to the licensee through a patent license to practice under the licensed patent within certain respects. The licensor can give or grant the licensee permission to make, use, sell, or import the patented invention. In granting a license, the licensor can do so on an "exclusive" or "nonexclusive" basis. Under an exclusive license, the licensor agrees to license the patented invention only to the licensee. The licensor also typically gives up his or her own right to practice the patented invention under an exclusive license. Thus, the patent owner, as licensor, must be keenly aware that the grant of an exclusive license will result in his or her inability to manufacture or sell the patented invention, unless such a right is expressly reserved by the licensor. In granting a license on a nonexclusive basis, the licensor remains free to grant licenses to others.

In addition to granting a license on an exclusive or nonexclusive basis, a licensor can also limit the license according to a specific activity known as "field of use" or "territory." For example, the patent license can be divided into the rights to make, to use, to sell, or to import. The license can grant the right to use, but not the right to make or sell. The field of use can also be divided. For example, an inventor of a patent on a drug can license the patent to one party to produce medicine for humans and to another party to produce medicine for animals. The inventor, as licensor, can also grant a patent license for a limited and specific geographic territory, such as by city, state, region, or country.

The licensor and licensee must also consider the duration of the patent license. The patent license can be for any period of time through the life of the patent. If the license does not specify the duration, the license is good for the term of the patent. In practical terms, duration is dependent on the life of the patent, the commercialization plans of the licensee, the market trends, and relative obsolescence of the patented technology. There are restrictions on the period for which royalties can be charged under a patent license. A patent license that provides for payment of royalties after the expiration of the patent would be in violation of the federal antitrust laws.

One of the paramount factors to a licensor in licensing his or her patent is the amount the licensor will be paid as consideration for the license grant. As mentioned earlier, payment to a licensor by a licensee in exchange for a license grant is typically in the form of a running royalty. A common question raised by most licensors in evaluating a patent license is, "What royalty should be charged?" There is generally no magic rate of royalty. The amount of royalty is determined by many factors that may include: the custom of the industry for which the patent or invention will be used; whether the licensee is getting an exclusive or nonexclusive license; whether the license includes other rights like trademarks, know-how, or technical assistance; whether the license limits the licensor's use of the patent or invention; and whether the size of the market for the invention and its pricing is sufficient to accommodate the royalty charged for the license.

Royalty payments are usually made on a "paid-up" basis or a "running-royalty" basis. A paid-up basis of payment for a license typically pays the licensor a one-time, lump-sum amount for an irrevocable license for the life of the patent. This is different from the running-royalty basis of payment, where payments are made over time usually as a percentage of the net sales of products covered by the licensed patent. Payment by the running-royalty basis can also include an up-front payment to the licensor, which may or may not be creditable against running royalties. Running royalties in patent licenses are usually structured as a percentage of defined net sales, net profits, or production output on a monthly, quarterly, semiannually, or other periodic basis.

It is also important that the licensor consider the following issues in structuring the royalty arrangement:
- the time and frequency of royalty payments,
- the requirement that the licensee keep accurate and complete accounting records,
- the right of the licensor to inspect the licensee's records,
- definition of the net sales or net profits against which the royalties are to be calculated, and
- the requirement that the licensee pay annual minimum royalties.

Many other terms and conditions can be included in the patent license, but the license must avoid provisions that violate the antitrust laws or constitute patent misuse. It has already been explained that a patent license cannot provide for royalty payments after the patent has expired. Additionally, the patent license must avoid illegal price fixing between the licensor and licensee and tying arrangements, such as where the licensee is required to purchase unpatented products from the licensor to maintain the patent license; this is considered patent misuse.

Selecting the right licensee is essential to being successful in licensing your patented invention. Grant licenses only to reputable companies that are seriously committed to commercializing and marketing the invention. Being viewed as a leader in a particular market or industry, possessing an entrepreneurial spirit, being receptive to new ideas, and having the demonstrated ability to successfully launch new products are attributes to considered in the selection of a licensee.

## Negotiating a Patent License

Even if the inventor is able to successfully prepare and prosecute a patent application, it may be more difficult for an inventor who is inexperienced in the art of negotiation and lacking in legal and business acumen to handle a transaction to license the invention. While licensing is presented as a basic procedure in this chapter, it can in practice be difficult and complex. To the extent that your licensing deal takes on complex issues different from those outlined in this chapter, it is advisable that you hire a patent attorney to assist in the structuring and review of your license transaction. If you have a good patent and an invention that is extremely marketable, you will find that any cost invested in hiring an attorney to assist in the protection of your interest at the negotiation table will far outweigh the agony of negotiating a bad deal on your own.

You negotiate every day; you negotiate anytime you deal with another person to obtain something that you want. You negotiate at work with supervisors, co-workers, customers, suppliers, government officials; at home with your spouse, parents, children, neighbors, and friends; and elsewhere with salespeople, auto dealers, merchants, and others. Being able to negotiate effectively is an important part of successfully licensing and profiting from your patented invention.

The ability to negotiate successfully requires creativity and good people skills. Negotiating also requires persistence, endurance, patience, organization, risk taking, vision, and high ethical values.

Nearly everyone can be an effective negotiator given the right preparation and knowledge of negotiating principles.

Three basic principles emerge from studying top negotiators. The first principle is "be soft on people, hard on ideas." This means that, as a negotiator, you should separate emotions from issues. This will help maintain a cooperative relationship between both parties. The second principle is "focus your attention on the major relevant issues and the desires and intentions behind the issues." The objective is to discover what each party really wants so that you can understand the actual needs of the parties and seek to create multiple options to help reach an agreement. The principle is to realize that there are many ways to reach a final agreement. The basis for successful negotiation is to be highly flexible and prolific in generating options.

Effective negotiation requires that the intentions of all the parties be acceptably satisfied. Initially, this element may seem ironic. How can everybody be satisfied? Somebody has to give while the other receives. According to traditional game theory, every gain by one party must equivalently correspond to a loss by the opposing party. While this outcome may apply to certain types of games, it has no place in successful negotiations.

Without planning and gathering information, you will be at a disadvantage in any negotiation. Nowhere is the saying "information is power" more emphatic than in the art of negotiation. All other things being equal, the negotiating party with the most knowledge and information about his or her opponent has the advantage.

Prepare for the license negotiations by establishing your opening, target, and bottom-line positions. Be ready to explain your positions and develop a good negotiating plan beforehand.

Start the negotiation process by establishing a positive climate. Be casual, friendly, and relaxed, and try to get the other party to do the same. Prepare an agenda and review the rules of the negotiation. Begin the negotiation by discussing and trying to reach agreement on minor issues. The major issues can be addressed later, when you and the other party have developed a rapport and a positive climate for negotiating. After both parties have outlined what they want out of the negotiations, begin generating options that will satisfy the interests of both parties.

Negotiate the patent license on the basis of some reasonable, customary, and objective standard apart from the emotional wills of the parties. Negotiating on the basis of standards that are fair and objective has several advantages, as it removes the battle for dominance that occurs in most negotiations where each party tries to force the other to back down from its position. This style of negotiating reduces the potential for escalating conflict. Even the parties cannot agree on what the objective standards should be, you can agree to search for some objective standards that are fair to both parties. This agreement alone represents a commitment to fairness that will enhance the working relationship between parties. In turn, this relationship improves the chances for an agreement that meets the interests of both parties. Using objective standards helps to ensure that neither party is shafted or taken. This, too, helps in preserving a working relationship and when long-term relationships are important to both parties.

In summary, step-by-step procedures for conducting and concluding successful negotiations include the following suggestions:

- establish a cooperative climate; agreeing on ground rules and an agenda; and identifying mutual outcomes;
- identify the problems and restate them in positive and resolvable terms;
- establish criteria by identifying outside objective standards and individual expectations;
- generate multiple options and evaluate these options using established criteria; agree on the best option for each issue; and then develop, enhance, and refine the best options;
- summarize specific areas of agreement to obtain closure; establish action plans and accountability to complete negotiations within the time allotted; summarize consequences and options if no agreement is reached; and
- acknowledge others participating in the negotiation and thank them for their contributions; reinforce the desire for a win-win situation and a long-term relationship.

## PATENT LICENSE AGREEMENT

1. Parties, Addresses, and Recitals
    1.1  THIS PATENT LICENSE AGREEMENT is made as of this _____day of
         _____, 199__ by and between _____ (hereinafter
         Licensor), at (Licensor's Address)_____, and
         _____(hereinafter Licensee)
         located at (Licensee's Address)_____. The parties
         agree as follows:
    1.2  Licensor is owner of United States Patent No. _____, granted
         _____ , 199__, covering the following invention:

    1.3  Licensee desires a (nonexclusive/exclusive) license under said United
         States Patent License No. _____.

2. Definitions
    2.1  Licensed Patent means United States Patent No. _____ granted on
         _____.

    2.2  Licensed Product means any product which is covered by any claim of the
         Licensed Patent or is made by a process or machine which, at the time
         of such making, is covered by any claim of the Licensed Patent.
    2.3  Net Selling Price in respect of Licensed Products sold means invoice price,
         after deduction of regular trade and quantity discounts, freight, insurance,
         taxes and agents' commissions where separately identified in the invoice.
         Where Licensed Products are not sold, but are otherwise disposed of, Net
         Selling Price for the purpose of computing royalties shall be the Net Selling
         Price at which products of similar kind and quality, sold in similar
         quantities, are currently being offered for sale by Licensee. Where such
         products are not currently being separately offered for sale by Licensee,
         the Net Selling Price of Licensed Products otherwise disposed of shall
         be Licensee's cost of manufacture, determined by Licensee's customary
         accounting procedures, increased by_____ percent (___%).

3. License Grant
    3.1  Licensor grants to Licensee a (nonexclusive/exclusive) license to make,
         use, sell, or import Licensed Product and to practice under the Licensed
         Product throughout the United States, its territories, and possessions.
    3.2  The term of the license granted to Licensee hereunder shall be for the
         full life of the Licensed Patent.

4. Royalties, Reports, and Payments

    4.1    Licensee shall pay royalties to Licensor on Licensed Products at the rate of _____ percent (__%) of the Net Selling Price of all such Licensed Products sold or otherwise disposed of by Licensee.

    4.2    Licensee shall make written reports to Licensor within thirty (30) days after the close of each calendar quarter stating in each such report the number, description, and aggregate Net Selling Price of Licensed Products sold or otherwise disposed of by Licensee during that calendar quarter.

            Concurrently with the making of each report, Licensee will pay to Licensor any and all royalties due and payable to Licensor on the Licensed Products included in the report.

    4.3    Licensee shall keep adequate and accurate records showing the Licensed Products sold or otherwise disposed of; such records are to be in sufficient detail to enable the royalties payable to Licensor to be determined. Licensee shall also permit his books and records to be examined from time to time to the extent necessary to verify the reports provided for in Section 4.2, such examination to be made at the expense of Licensor by an independent auditor appointed by Licensor who shall report to Licensor only the amount of royalty payable for the period under audit.

5. Representations and Warranties; Limitations

    5.1    Licensor and Licensee each represents that he or she has the legal right to enter into this Patent License Agreement and to carry out his or her obligations hereunder.

    5.2    Nothing in this Patent License Agreement shall be construed as:

        (a) A warranty or representation by either party as to the validity or scope of any Licensed Patent; or

        (b) A warranty or representation that anything made, used, sold, or otherwise disposed of under any license granted in this Agreement is or will be free from infringement of patents of third persons; or

        (c) A requirement that either party shall file any patent application, secure any patent, or maintain any patent in force; or

        (d) An obligation to bring or prosecute actions or suits against third parties for infringement of any patent; or

        (e) An obligation to furnish any manufacturing or technical information, or any information concerning pending patent applications; or

        (f) Conferring a right to use in advertising, publicity, or otherwise any trademark or trade name of the party from which a license is received under the Agreement; or

        (g) Granting by implication, estoppel, or otherwise, any licenses or rights under patents other than the Licensed Patent.

5.3 Neither party makes any representations, extends any warranties of any kind, either express or implied, or assumes any responsibilities whatever with respect to use, sale, or other disposition by the other party or its vendees or transferees of products incorporating or made by use of inventions licensed under this Patent License Agreement.

6. Transferability of Rights and Obligations

6.1 The license or release granted in this Patent License Agreement by Licensor in respect to the Licensed Patent shall be binding upon any successor of the Licensor in ownership or control of the Licensed Patent.

6.2 The obligations of Licensee to make reports, pay royalties, and maintain records under this Agreement shall run in favor of any person or legal entity which is a successor or assignee of Licensor in respect to Licensor's benefits under this Patent License Agreement.

6.3 The license granted to Licensee under this Patent License Agreement shall pass to any assigns for the benefit of creditors of the licensed party, and to any receiver of its assets, or to any person or corporation succeeding to its entire business in Licensed Products as a result of sale, consolidation, reorganization, or otherwise, provided such assignee, receiver, person, or legal entity shall, promptly, accept in writing the provisions of this Agreement and agree to become in all respects bound thereby in the place and stead of the Licensee, but this Patent License Agreement and Licensee's obligations hereunder may not otherwise be transferred without the written consent of the Licensor.

7. Terms and Termination

7.1 Unless otherwise terminated as provided in Section 7.2, this agreement shall remain in effect until the date of expiration of the Licensed Patents and shall thereupon terminate.

7.2 Licensor may terminate this Patent License Agreement at any time in the event of a default by Licensee in the due observance or performance of any covenant, condition, or limitation of this Patent License Agreement required to be performed by Licensee, but only if Licensee has not remedied its default within thirty (30) days after receipt from Licensee of written notice of such default.

8. Notices; Applicable Law; Arbitration

8.1 Any notice, report, or payment provided for in this Agreement shall be deemed sufficiently given when sent by certified or registered mail addressed to the party for whom intended at the address given at the beginning of this Agreement or at such changed address as the party shall have specified by written notice.

8.2   This Agreement shall be construed, interpreted, and applied in accordance with the laws of the State of _____.

8.3   Any controversy or claim arising under or related to this Patent License Agreement shall be settled by binding arbitration in accordance with the Rules of the American Arbitration Association before a single arbitrator selected in accordance with those rules, and judgment upon the award rendered by the arbitrator may be entered in any court having jurisdiction thereof.

9. Entire Agreement

9.1   This Agreement contains the entire and only agreement between the parties and supersedes all preexisting Agreements between them respecting its subject matter. Any representation, promise, or condition in connection with such subject matter which is not incorporated in this Agreement shall not be binding upon either party. No modification, renewal, extension, waive, and (except as provided in Article VII hereof) no termination of this Agreement or any of its provisions shall be binding upon the party against whom enforcement of such modification, renewal, extension, waiver, or termination is sought, unless made in writing and signed on behalf of such party by one of its executive officers. As used herein, the word "termination" includes any and all means of bringing to an end prior to its expiration by its own terms this Agreement, or any provision thereof, whether by release, discharge, abandonment, or otherwise.

IN WITNESS WHEREOF, each of the parties has caused this Agreement to be executed and duly sealed in duplicate originals by its duly authorized representative.

LICENSOR                                    LICENSEE

By: _____        By: _____

Date: _____        Date: _____

# Starting a Business to Market Your Invention

ONE APPROACH TO COMMERCIALIZING your ideas or inventions is to start your own business. You may want to do all or part of the manufacturing, distribution, and marketing yourself. This approach can be difficult and time consuming, but it can also be the most rewarding. This chapter provides essential information for evaluating and implementing your skills and resources in starting you own business.

## Evaluating Yourself as a Business Owner

Entrepreneurship may not be for everyone. You may not have the characteristics of a true entrepreneur, and you may not want to invest the time and resources that a successful business requires. To be sure about entrepreneurship, study the characteristics of successful business owners to see if you have the right traits.

Studies have shown that entrepreneurs are generally people who have high initiative, are self-confident, set long-term goals, are able to solve problems, take appropriate risks, learn from mistakes, and use all available resources. They compete with themselves and believe that success or failure lies within their personal control and influence.

Answering some basic questions about your abilities and your business endeavors can provide reality testing for your ideas. You can order a copy of the pamphlet *Checklist for Going into Business* from the SBA. Answer the questions and discuss your answers with friends and family. Or better yet, ask several people, who know you well, to think carefully about you and answer the checklist for you. Have you under- or overestimated your abilities? Sometimes an evaluation by a friend is more useful than a self-evaluation.

The SBA offers many publications and other sources of information that may be useful to you in starting a new business. The following pamphlets are available for a small fee by writing to the Small Business Administration, P.O. Box 15436, Fort Worth, TX 76119:

- *Thinking About Going into Business* (MA 2.025)
- *Checklist for Going into Business* (MA 2.016)
- *Ideas into Dollars* (SBB 91)
- *Selecting the Legal Structure for Your Business* (MA 6.004)
- *Marketing for Small Business* (SBB 89)
- *Keeping Records in Small Business* (MA 1.017)

Before starting your own business, think about what resources are available to you. Will you start by keeping your job and moonlighting for a while? Do you have a small nest egg, inheritance, or retirement income to live on until you get the business going? Do you have a network of contacts and possible customers through your previous lines of work, or will you be starting from scratch? Answering these questions honestly and completely will help you assess the chances of success with a new business idea.

## Examining Your Business Idea

Now that you have come up with an invention or business idea, consider the following questions: Are there customers for my product or service? How do I know there are customers? How will I find them? Who are my competitors? What will I charge for my product or service? How will I promote my product or service? Finding the answers to these questions is the challenging and sometimes tedious homework that will help you determine your chances for success, and whether you should look for another, more marketable idea. Keep in mind that a person may be able to start and operate a business, particularly a part-time one, out of his or her home.

Developing a professional image may be hard if you work out of your home. Projecting a businesslike image is an important part of building credibility with your customers and contributing to your own professional self-image. Design a logo or have one designed, and order business cards and stationery. Set regular business hours. Use an answering machine or answering service. If other members of the family also answer the phone, make sure they know what to say. Have a businesslike office or showroom if meeting customers face to face. Consider referring to the apartment number as "suite number" or rent a post office box. Such practices might improve the chance of doing business with potential customers.

The first step in creating a business is to decide what your product or service is. What are you selling? Write a short, specific statement describing your product or service. Getting a clear idea of a business concept is one of the most difficult tasks in creating a business. The statement may change several times as you experiment with the market and test your skills. Describe the product or service to family, friends, potential customers, and fellow businesspeople. Is the description clear and brief? Can you say it with confidence and enthusiasm?

Answer the question, "Who will buy my product or service?" to develop and test your business idea. Make a list of potential customers, such as individuals, groups, segments of the population, or other businesses, that need the product or service. Ask friends and colleagues for help in brainstorming potential customers, markets, and uses for your product or service.

Your business planning must also include an up-to-date analysis of the competition. Analysis of the competition is important to help you plan your market position—how you will fit into the market-place. Will the product or service be cheaper or more expensive than that of the major competitors? Will it be more durable? What benefits can be built into the product or service that the competitors don't offer? In planning your business, look for a unique product or niche that will give freedom from strong competition or that will make the product or service more valuable than others in the market.

As a new business owner becoming more familiar with the competition, you will also be discovering where and how to find customers. Whatever the type of business you want to open, you will need to do market research to determine if there are buyers for your idea, where they are, and how to find them. And in the process, you will also be gathering information on pricing and competition. The more you learn about the competition, the better you will be able to decide how to position yourself in the market.

Visit the local library to compile local and county statistics on the size and makeup of the market. While at the library, check out books on marketing research. Also, check the following resources that might have data about the product or service or the people who would use it:

- *Encyclopedia of Associations*, 17th Edition. Gale Research Company, Book Tower, Detroit, MI 48226.
- *Ayer Directory of Publications*. Lists trade publications by subject matter. Contact the sales, marketing, or research departments for buying patterns among their readers.
- "Survey of Buying Power." *Sales, Marketing, Management* magazine. July issue each year.
- *Thomas Register*. Lists companies by product and service line, organized geographically and alphabetically.
- *Directory of Business, Trade, and Public Policy Organizations*. U.S. Small Business Administration, Office of Advocacy.
- Publications of the Department of Commerce. Data User Series Division, Bureau of the Census, Washington, D.C. 20233.
- *County Business Patterns*. U.S. Department of Commerce, Bureau of the Census. Available for each state.

Newspaper ads and trade magazines are other good sources of market information. Check also with the Chamber of Commerce, the county office of economic development, the census bureau, and businesses and professional organizations to gather market and pricing data.

Finding money to finance your new business idea can be your biggest obstacle. Most banks and financial institutions will be unwilling to lend money for a new and untested idea. You will have to rely on your own funds to a large extent to start your new business, or you may perhaps turn to a venture capitalist.

Calculate how much money it would take to develop your idea for commercialization, to set up the new business, and to operate it for two to three years. This amount will likely be your minimum capital requirements. Then, see if you can meet these requirements from your personal savings or access to credit. Consider loans from your credit union or employer's 401(k) savings plan as relatively easy sources of credit.

Prepare a professional business plan that describes your product or service, analyzes the potential markets and customers, reviews the competitive situation, and spells out your marketing strategy.

Form a network of friends and business associates, if necessary, and have them invest money and services in your new business in exchange for part ownership. Create a network of people with diverse professional skills to handle the various technical, legal, financial, and marketing issues for your new business.

Venture capitalists are typically willing to take on the risks of financing promising new ideas. They may, however, want control of the business and a large share of the profits. You can find sources to venture capitalists at your libraries and universities. For less than $100.00, you can obtain information on venture capitalists by calling the Venture Capital Hotline at (408) 625-0700. To seek venture capital, you will need to prepare a good business plan that explains your business idea, the funding requirements, and its market potential.

When the marketing research is completed, it will have identified potential customers; helped discover their habits, needs, preferences, and buying cycles; and provided insight on how to reach them to generate sales.

Promotion is an overall, long-range plan designed to inform potential customers about what is being sold. Advertising is usually thought of as the paid communication part of the promotion program.

Answer these questions to develop a total promotional campaign:

(1) What image or message do I want to promote? (2) What are the best media and activities for reaching my potential customers? (3) How much time and money can I spend on the effort?

Develop a long-range, consistent program for building image and reaching customers. Your image should be reflected in your business card, logo, stationery, brochure, newsletter, telephone answering service, signs, paid ads, and promotional activities.

Several small ads may have more impact than one large, splashy ad. Conduct a campaign rather than having a one-shot ad or event. If hiring a public relations firm, look for one that gives personal attention and develops a total marketing plan, not just a couple of ads. The plan should include market research, a profile of the target audience, a clear description of the image you want to project, the written copy, and a list of media (including cost and scheduling calendars) that are best for your product or service. Most new, small business owners will probably want to set aside a certain dollar amount per year or a percentage of past, current, or projected sales for paid advertising.

## Choosing Your Form of Business Organization

One of the most important decisions a business owner will make is whether to set up the business as a sole proprietorship, a partnership, or a corporation. Note, however, that as a small business owner, you essentially risk it all, no matter what form of business organization you choose. Although most small businesses are sole proprietorships or partnerships, a comparison of the advantages and disadvantages of each type of organization should be made.

A sole proprietorship is the least costly way of starting a business. You can form a sole proprietorship by finding a location and opening the door for business. There are the usual fees for registering the business name and for legal work in changing zoning restrictions and obtaining necessary licenses. Attorney's fees for starting a sole proprietorship will be less than for the other forms because less document preparation is required.

Here are some advantages and disadvantages of the sole proprietorship:

| ADVANTAGES | DISADVANTAGES |
|---|---|
| Easiest to get started | Unlimited liability |
| Greatest freedom of action | Death or illness endanger business |
| Maximum authority | Growth limited to owner's energies |
| Income tax advantages in very small firms | Personal affairs easily mixed with business |
| Social security advantage to owner | |

A partnership can be formed by simply making an oral agreement between two or more persons, although such informality is not recommended. Legal fees for drawing up a partnership agreement are higher than those for a sole proprietorship, but the fees may be lower than those for incorporating. Partners would be wise, however, to consult an attorney to have a partnership agreement drafted to help resolve future disputes.

Here are some advantages and disadvantages of the partnership form of business:

| ADVANTAGES | DISADVANTAGES |
|---|---|
| Two heads better than one | Difficult to transfer interest |
| Additional sources of venture capital | Death, withdrawal, or bankruptcy of one partner endangers business |
| Better credit rating than corporation of similar size | Personal liability for partnership obligations |
| | Difficult to get rid of bad partner |
| | Hazy line of authority |

A special form of business organization is the limited partnership, which combines features of a general partnership and a corporation. With this form, there must always be at least one general partner who remains personally liable for partnership liabilities. The limited partners are usually only liable up to the extent of their investment in the limited partnership. This exemption from personal liability normally continues as long as the limited partner does not participate in the management or control of the business. As many complex issues may arise with a limited partnership, it is recommended that legal counsel be obtained.

A corporation is the most complex form of business, and statutory requirements must be met to bring it into existence. A corporation is a separate legal entity that is established pursuant to state law. As a separate legal entity, a corporation can contract in its own name, hold property in its own name, and can sue and be sued in court in its own name.

The formation of a corporation requires the preparation of Articles of Incorporation, which are filed with the Secretary of State for the state where the corporation is being formed. The Articles of Incorporation usually include the name of the corporation, its location and registered agent, its purposes, the amount and classes of stocks, the first board of directors, and the names and addresses of the incorporators. Generally, once the Articles of Incorporation are filed and approved by the Secretary of State, the corporation comes into existence.

You can incorporate without an attorney, but it may be unwise to do so. People may think a small family corporation does not need an attorney, but an attorney can save members of a family corporation from hard feelings and family squabbles. Attorney's fees can be expensive if organization problems are complex. The corporate form of business is usually the most costly to organize.

Here are some advantages and disadvantages of the corporate form of business:

| ADVANTAGES | DISADVANTAGES |
|---|---|
| Limited liability for stockholders (while true for big business, may not be for small business) | Gives owner a false sense of security |
| | Heavier taxes |
| | Power limited by the charter |
| Continuity | Less freedom of activity |
| Transfer of shares | Legal formalities |
| Easier to raise capital | More expensive to launch |
| Possible to separate business functions into different corporations | |

A corporation is generally taxed as a separate entity, and shareholders are also taxed on corporate income paid to them as dividends. The election of Subchapter S status, however, allows an eligible corporation to escape the double taxation. The purpose of Subchapter S is to permit a "small business corporation" to elect to have its income taxed to the shareholders as if the corporation were a partnership. Subchapter S status overcomes the double taxation of corporate income and permits the shareholders to have the benefit of offsetting business losses by the corporation against the income of the shareholders. An election for Subchapter S status requires that the corporation file Form 2553 with the Internal Revenue Service.

## Laws Affecting Your Business

Most localities have registration and licensing requirements that will apply to business owners. A license is a formal permission to practice a certain business activity, issued by a local, state, or federal government. The activities may be the type of business that requires a permit from the local authorities. There is often a small fee for licenses and permits (usually $15.00 to $25.00). A license may require an examination to certify that the recipient is qualified. The business name must usually be registered, and an appropriate tax number must be obtained. Separate business telephones and bank accounts are recommended. If there are employees, the business owner is responsible for withholding income and social security taxes. The business owner is also responsible for paying worker's compensation and unemployment insurance and complying with minimum wage and employee health laws.

If your operations are intrastate, you will be concerned primarily with state and local, rather than federal, licensing. Businesses frequently subject to state or local control are retail food establishments, nightclubs and taverns, barber shops, beauty shops, plumbing firms, and taxi companies. These are primarily service businesses and are subject to regulations for the protection of public health and morals. An attorney can help make sure that you have complied with all licensing and permit requirements. Depending on the type of business, you may have to comply with building and safety codes too.

Think twice about the liabilities of operating without proper licenses and registrations. If you begin to advertise or are in the news, you will probably hear from a local official. You will pay with embarrassment, time, and money if your business is not properly licensed.

If you find legal regulations, permits, and licenses confusing, make sure you find some way to get the information you need in order to operate legally. You can get help from your attorney, accountant, business partner, or even your local librarian. Complying with legal regulations is not an aspect of business operations that can be delayed until you "get around to it." Your business reputation and financial standing are at stake.

## Working with Professionals

Even the smallest and newest business needs help from at least two kinds of specialists, an attorney and an accountant. Depending on the type of business and your skills, from time to time, you may need the advice of your professionals, such as a direct-mail or marketing specialist, an insurance representative, management consultant, a computer specialist, a realtor, or a public relations expert.

Several guidelines will hold true no matter what type of expert you are dealing with. Interview professionals to see if you will be comfortable working with them. Make sure they provide the service you need, agree on the working relationship, and state appropriate fees. Be completely honest about your business situation. Advice based on partial or incorrect information is no advice at all. If the business is having problems, don't be embarrassed. If the sales are down, give the experts all the available information and work as a team to solve the problem. If business is good, don't be afraid that professionals will steal ideas or expect a raise. Build a trusting, businesslike relationship. Expect the professionals to spend some of the time teaching and explaining complex concepts. But don't expect to be spoon-fed decisions or to delegate all decisions to them. Take a course at the local community college in record keeping and taxes or in public relations to develop more skill in your areas of inexperience. Keep appointments and pay bills promptly.

To find an attorney who is familiar with businesses of your size and type, ask for referrals from business colleagues, your accountants, the local Chamber of Commerce, your bankers, or some other trusted source. Some local bar associations run an attorney referral and information service. Some services provide only names, and others give information on experience and fees to help match needs to the attorney's background and charges.

An attorney can help decide which is the most advantageous business structure (sole proprietorship, partnership, or corporation). He or she can help with zoning, permit, or licensing problems; health inspection problems; unpaid bills, contracts, and agreements; patents, trademarks, and copyright protection; and some tax problems. Because there is always the possibility of a lawsuit, claim, or other legal action against your business, it is wise to have an attorney who is already familiar with the business before a crisis arises. An attorney experienced with your type of venture could also advise on laws, programs, and agencies—federal, state, or local— that help small businesses through loans, grants, procurement set- asides, counseling, and in other ways. He or she can tell you about unexpected legal opportunities and pitfalls that can affect the business.

In choosing an attorney, his or her experience and fees should be related. One attorney may charge an hourly rate that, at first, looks cheaper than that of another. However, because of a lack of experience in some area, the less expensive attorney may charge a larger fee by the time the service is provided. Ask your attorney for a résumé and check with references. If you feel overwhelmed with the process, take a trusted friend to the initial meeting to help you keep on track as you interview the attorney about services and fees.

If a law firm is retained, be sure to understand who will work on the case and who will supervise the work. If junior attorneys handle the work, the fees should be lower. This arrangement is usually fine as long as an experienced attorney reviews the case periodically.

Tell the attorney that you expect to be informed of all develop- ments and consulted before any decisions are made. You may also want to receive copies of all documents, letters, and memos written and received in the case or have a chance to read them in the attorney's office.

Ask the attorney to estimate the timetable and costs of the work. You may consider placing a periodic ceiling on fees, after which the attorney will call before proceeding to do work that would add to the bill. Always have a written retainer agreement describing what you and your attorney expect of each other.

Most businesses fail not for lack of good ideas or good will, but rather for lack of financial expertise and planning. Look for an accountant as you would an attorney. Get referrals from trusted friends, business associations, or professional organizations. Discuss fees in advance and draw up a written agreement about how you will work together. Accountants (along with an attorney) can advise about initial business decisions, such as the form of the business. They can also help set up the books, draw up and analyze profit and loss statements, advise on financial decisions, and give advice on cash requirements for the start-up phase. Accountants can make budget forecasts, help prepare financial information for a loan application, and handle tax matters.

Accounting firms offer a variety of services. If accounting is not an easy area for you as a business owner, the fees you pay will be well worth it. Most accounting firms maintain books of original entry, prepare bank reconciliation statements and post the general ledger, prepare balance sheets and income statements on a quarterly or semiannual basis, and design and implement various accounting and record keeping systems. They will also get federal and state withholding numbers, give instructions on where and when to file tax returns, prepare tax returns, and do general tax planning for the small business owner.

As a business owner, your accountant is your key financial advisor. The accountant should alert you to potential danger areas, advise you on how to handle growth spurts, help you to best plan for times of slow business, and direct you on how to financially nurture and protect your business future.

## Maintaining Your Business Records

Keeping accurate and up-to-date business records is, for many people, the most difficult and uninteresting aspect of operating a small business. If this area of business management is one that you anticipate will be hard for you, plan now for how you will cope with it. Don't wait until tax time or until business transactions are totally confused. Take a course on record keeping at the local community college, ask a volunteer SCORE® (Service Corps of Retired Executives) representative from the SBA to help you in the beginning, or hire an accountant to give you advice on setting up and maintaining a record keeping system.

Business records will be used to prepare tax returns, make business decisions, and apply for loans. Set aside a special time each day to update business records. Keeping up-to-date, accurate records will pay off in the long run with more deductions and fewer headaches.

If the business is small or related to an activity that is usually considered a hobby, it's even more important that good records be kept. The Internal Revenue Service may decide that the activity is only a hobby, and deductions for expenses or losses from income produced at home would not be allowed at tax time. So, as a business owner, keep records of all transactions which include spending or earning money.

The business records should tell how much cash is owed, how much cash is due, and how much cash is on hand. A business owner should keep these basic records:

- Check register to record each check disbursed, the date of disbursement, number of the check, to whom it was made out (payee), the amount of money disbursed, and for what purpose.
- Cash receipts to shows the amount of money received from whom and for what.
- Sales journal to record each business transaction, the date of the transaction, for whom it was performed, the amount of the invoice, and the sales tax, if applicable. The journal may be divided to indicate labor and goods.
- Voucher register to record bills, money owed, the date of the bill, to whom it is owed, the amount owed, and for what service.
- General journal as a means of adjusting some entries in the other four journals.

Business records should be set up to reflect the amount and type of activity in the particular business. There are a wide range of prepackaged record keeping systems. The pamphlet *Small Business*

*Bibliography* (No. 15) from the SBA lists many such systems. The most useful system for a small business is usually based on what is called the One-Write System. It captures information at the time the transaction takes place. One-Write Systems are efficient because they eliminate the need for recopying the data and are compatible with electronic data processing if the business is computerized.

Even though the business may be small and just beginning, it is wise to consult an accountant to help decide which record keeping system is best for the business. Once it is set up, record the daily transactions in the general ledger and prepare financial statements for the business.

Establish a separate bank account for the business—even before the first sale. Then you will have a complete and distinct record of your income and expenditures for tax purposes, and you won't have to remember which expenses were business and which were personal.

Choosing a record keeping system you understand and will use is important. The records will help you see how well the business is doing, which is the first step in responsible financial management.

## Learning from Experience and Networking

Successful business owners learn from experience—their own experiences and those of others. In a study of entrepreneurial personality characteristics, it was noted that successful entrepreneurs are disappointed but not discouraged by failure. They use failures as learning experiences and try to understand their role in causing the failure in order to avoid similar problems in the future. Furthermore, the study found that entrepreneurs seek and use feedback on their performance in order to take corrective action and improve.

As an entrepreneur, you can learn from experience in several ways. You can work closely and creatively with professional advisors, such as your attorney and accountant. As you continually review your business records, you will see "mistakes," but you will also begin to develop skill in planning and managing.

You will continue to learn about all areas of business operations, constantly acquiring new ideas. Most community colleges have short, inexpensive, practical courses for business owners in topics like Financing Small Business, Choosing a Small Business Computer, and Starting and Operating a Home-Based Business.

Get to know other business owners with similar needs or problems. Talking with others can be a way to avoid repeating the mistakes they have made and to benefit from their experience. Local and national organizations offer memberships, social events, networking opportunities, newsletters, and seminars for small business owners. Advertise your product or service to other business owners through these organizations. They can also provide a way to learn about services you may need, such as accounting, public relations, or a responsible secretarial service. These organizations may offer updates in such areas as taxes and zoning in their newsletters and workshops.

Whatever the current business problems, there is likely to be a solution. Somewhere there is information, a book, a person, an organization, or a government agency that can help. A word of warning though: finding resources and building networks can be very time consuming. Joining organizations can turn out to be expensive, especially if you are too busy to use their services and support once you join.

Use the following list or organize a search for useful resources, then pick and choose carefully what to read, join, buy, or attend.

- The Public Library: Visit the local library and become familiar with its resources. In addition to books, many libraries offer free workshops, lend skill-building tapes, and are a place to pick up catalogs and brochures describing continuing education opportunities for business owners. Ask the librarian for current copies of zoning regulations. Become familiar with new books and resources in pertinent fields (e.g., computers, health care, or crafts) as well as in business skills (e.g., advertising techniques, or financing). Look for magazines such as *In Business, Black Enterprise, Venture*, or *Journal of Small Business Management*. Reading selectively is free. Subscribing to too many magazines may be expensive.

- Organizations: A wide variety of local and national organizations have sprung up to serve the informational, lobbying, and networking needs of business entrepreneurs. Through meetings, services, or newsletters, groups such as the National

Association of Women Business Owners, American Entrepreneurs Association, Business of Professional Women's Club, National Alliance of Home-Based Businesswomen, and the National Association for Cottage Industry offer members everything from camaraderie to valuable "perks," such as group rates on health insurance. David Gumpert's book, *The Insider's Guide to Small Business Resources*, has addresses of many of these groups and other information on such resources.

- Government Resources: Contact the local or district office of the SBA to learn about its services and publications. The SBA also offers free or inexpensive workshops and counseling through SCORE®. As mentioned earlier, SCORE® is a volunteer program sponsored by the SBA through which retired executives who have management expertise are linked with owners and managers of small businesses or prospective entrepreneurs who need help.

- Additional Government Resources: The Department of Commerce, Bureau of the Census, Department of Defense (procurement), Department of Labor, Internal Revenue Service (ask for the free Business Tax Kit), FTC, and the GPO all have publications and services to inform and support small businesses. Local and state government offices may also provide services and assistance. Addresses are available in the telephone book under U.S. Government, at the public library, or at the SBA office.

- Community Colleges: Most community colleges offer short, inexpensive, noncredit programs for entrepreneurs. The classes usually are convenient for business owners and are taught by experienced owners and managers.

If you are an owner of a small business, particularly if you operate from your home, you can overcome feelings of isolation and give and receive valuable information through networks and other resources. Being active in professional and trade associations will help to build a good marketing network for the business' service or product. Take the time and invest the money for memberships. Then, continually evaluate which organizations and resources best serve your business information and networking needs.

# Appendix

## 1. 35 United States Code

§ 101.    Inventions patentable

Whoever invents or discovers any new and useful process, machine, manufacture, or composition of matter, or any new and useful improvement thereof, may obtain a patent therefor, subject to the conditions and requirements of this title.

§ 102.    Conditions for patentability, novelty, and loss or right to patent

A person shall be entitled to a patent unless—

(a)  the invention was known or used by others in this country or was patented or was described in a printed publication in this or a foreign country, before the invention thereof by the applicant for patent; or

(b)  the invention was patented or described in a printed publication in this or a foreign country or in public use or on sale in this country, more than one year prior to the date of the application for patent in the United States; or

(c)  he has abandoned the invention; or

(d)  the invention was first patented or caused to be patented, or was the subject of an inventor's certificate, by the applicant or his legal representatives or assigns in a foreign country prior to the date of the application for patent in this country on an application for patent or inventor's certificate filed more than twelve months before the filing of the application in the United States; or

(e)  the invention was described in a patent granted on an application for patent by another filed in the United States before the invention thereof by the applicant for patent, or on an international application by another who has fulfilled the requirements of paragraphs (1), (2), and (4) of Section 371(c) of this title before the invention thereof by the applicant for patent; or

(f) he did not himself invent the subject matter sought to be patented; or

(g) before the applicant's invention thereof the invention was made in this country by another who has not abandoned, suppressed, or concealed it. In determining priority of invention there shall be considered not only the respective dates of conception and reduction to practice of the invention, but also the reasonable diligence of one who was first to conceive and last to reduce to practice, from a time prior to conception by the other.

§ 103.    Conditions for patentability, nonobvious subject matter

A patent may not be obtained though the invention is not identically disclosed or described as set forth in Section 102 of this title, if the differences between the subject matter sought to be patented and the prior art are such that the subject matter as a whole would have been obvious at the time the invention was made to a person having ordinary skill in the art to which said subject matter pertains. Patentability shall not be negatived by the manner in which the invention was made.

Subject matter developed by another person, which qualifies as prior art only under subsection (f) or (g) of Section 102 of this title, shall not preclude patentability under this section where the subject matter and the claimed invention were, at the time the invention was made, owned by the same person or subject to an obligation of assignment to the same person.

§ 112.    Specification

This specification shall contain a written description of the invention, and of the manner and process of making and using it, in such full, clear, concise, and exact terms as to enable any person skilled in the art to which it pertains, or with which it is most nearly connected, to make and use the same, and shall set forth the best mode contemplated by the inventor of carrying out his invention.

The specification shall conclude with one or more claims particularly pointing out and distinctly claiming the subject matter which the applicant regards as his invention.

§ 271. Infringement of patent

(a) Except as otherwise provided in this title, whoever without authority makes, uses, offers to sell, or sells any patented invention within the United States or imports into the United States any patented invention during the term of the patent therefor, infringes the patent.

(b) Whoever actively induces infringement of a patent shall be liable as an infringer.

(c) Whoever offers to sell or sells within the United States or imports into the United State a component of a patented machine, manufacture, combination or composition, or a material or apparatus for use in practicing a patented process, constituting a material part of the invention, knowing the same to be especially made or especially adapted for use in an infringement of such patent, and not a staple article or commodity of commerce suitable for substantial non-infringing use, shall be liable as a contributory infringer.

(d) No patent owner otherwise entitled to relief for infringement or contributory infringement of a patent shall be denied relief or deemed guilty of misuse or illegal extension of the patent right by reason of his having done one or more of the following: (1) derived revenue from acts which if performed by another without his consent would constitute contributory infringement of the patent; (2) licensed or authorized another to perform acts which if performed without his consent would constitute contributory infringement of the patent; (3) sought to enforce his patent rights against infringement or contributory infringement; (4) refused to license or use any rights to the patent; or (5) conditioned the license of any rights to the patent or sale of the patented product on the acquisition of a license to rights in another patent or purchase of a separate product, unless, in view of the circumstances, the patent owner has market power in the relevant market for the patent or patented product on which the license or sale is conditioned.

(e) (1) It shall not be an act of infringement to make, use, offer to sell, or sell within the United States or import into the United States a patented invention (other than a new animal drug or veterinary biological product (as those terms are used in the Federal Food, Drug, and Cosmetic Act and the Act of March 4, 1913) which is primarily manufactured using recombinant DNA, recombinant RNA, hybridoma technology, or other processes involving site specific genetic manipulation techniques) solely for uses reasonably related to the development and submission of information under a federal law which regulates the manufacture, use, or sale of drugs or veterinary biological products . . .

(f) (1) Whoever without authority supplies or causes to be supplied in or from the United States all or a substantial portion of the components of a patented invention, where such components are uncombined in whole or in part, in such manner as to actively induce the combination of such components outside of the United States in a manner that would infringe the patent if such combination occurred within the United States, shall be liable as an infringer.

(2) Whoever without authority supplies or causes to be supplied in or from the United States any component of a patented invention that is especially made or especially adapted for use in the invention and

not a staple article or commodity of commerce suitable for substantial noninfringing use, where such component is uncombined in whole or in part, knowing that such component is so made or adapted and intending that such component will be combined outside of the United States in a manner that would infringe the patent if such combination occurred within the United States, shall be liable as an infringer.

(g) Whoever without authority imports into the United States or offers to sell, sells, or uses within the United States a product which is made by a process patented in the United States shall be liable as an infringer, if the importation, offer to sell, sale, or use of the product occurs during the term of such process patent. In an action for infringement of a process patent, no remedy may be granted for infringement on account of the noncommercial use or retail sale of a product unless there is no adequate remedy under this title for infringement on account of the importation or other use, offer to sell, or sale of that product. A product which is made by a patented process will, for purposes of this title, not be considered to be so made after: (1) it is materially changed by subsequent processes; or (2) it becomes a trivial and nonessential component of another product.

### § 284. Damages

Upon finding for the claimant the court shall award the claimant damages adequate to compensate for the infringement but in no event less than a reasonable royalty for the use made of the invention by the infringer, together with interest and costs as fixed by the court. When the damages are not found by a jury, the court shall assess them. In either event the court may increase the damages up to three times the amount found or assessed. The court may receive expert testimony as an aid to the determination of damages or of what royalty would be reasonable under the circumstances.

### § 285. Attorney fees

The court in exceptional cases may award reasonable attorney fees to the prevailing party.

## 2. PTO Fees

The U.S. Patent and Trademark Office has amended its rules or practice in patent cases, Part 1 of Title 37, Code of Federal Regulations to adjust certain patent fee amounts to reflect fluctuations in the Consumer Price Index (CPI).

Any fee payment due and paid on or after October 1, 1997, must be paid in the revised amount. The date of mailing indicated on a proper Certificate of Mailing or Transmission under 37 C.F.R. § 1.8 will be considered to be the date of receipt and payment in the Office.

As this fee sheet is a summary and the content of rules also may be changing, you should refer to the notice published in the *Official Gazette of the United States Patent and Trademark Office* of August 19, 1997. The fees, which are subject to reduction for small entities who have established status (37 C.F.R. § 1.27), are shown in a separate column.

For additional information, please contact the PTO General Information Services Division at (800) PTO-9199 or (703) 308-4357.

| DESCRIPTION | FEE | SMALL ENTITY FEE (IF APPLICABLE) |
|---|---|---|
| **PATENT FILING FEES** | | |
| Basic filing fee: utility | 790.00 | 395.00 |
| Independent claims in excess of three | 82.00 | 41.00 |
| Claims in excess of twenty | 22.00 | 11.00 |
| Multiple dependent claim | 270.00 | 135.00 |
| Surcharge: Late filing fee or oath or declaration | 130.00 | 65.00 |
| Design filing fee | 330.00 | 165.00 |
| Plant filing fee | 540.00 | 270.00 |
| Provisional application filing fee | 150.00 | 75.00 |
| Non-English specification | 130.00 | |
| **PATENT ISSUE FEES** | | |
| Utility issue fee | 1,320.00 | 660.00 |
| Design issue fee | 450.00 | 225.00 |
| Plant issue fee | 670.00 | 335.00 |
| **PATENT MAINTENANCE FEES** *(Application filed on or after December 12, 1980)* | | |
| Due at 3.5 years | 1,050.00 | 525.00 |
| Due at 7.5 years | 2,100.00 | 1,050.00 |
| Due at 11.5 years | 3,160.00 | 1,580.00 |
| Surcharge: Late payment within 6 months | 130.00 | 65.00 |
| Surcharge after expiration: Late payment is unavoidable | 680.00 | |
| Surcharge after expiration: Late payment is unintentional | 1,600.00 | |
| **MISCELLANEOUS PATENT FEES** | | |
| For filing a request for reexamination | 2,520.00 | |
| Statutory Disclaimer | 110.00 | 55.00 |
| Extension for response within first month | 110.00 | 55.00 |
| Extension for response within second month | 400.00 | 200.00 |
| Extension for response within third month | 950.00 | 475.00 |
| Extension for response within fourth month | 1,510.00 | 755.00 |
| Extension for response within fifth month | 2,060.00 | 1,030.00 |
| Notice of appeal | 310.00 | 155.00 |
| Filing a brief in support of an appeal | 310.00 | 155.00 |

Request for oral hearing ...................................................... 270.00 ............. 135.00
Petitions to the Commissioner, unless otherwise specified ..... 130.00
Submission of an Information Disclosure
  Statement (§ 1.97(c)) ......................................................... 240.00
Petition to institute a public use proceeding ...................... 1,510.00
Petition to revive unavoidably abandoned application ........ 110.00 ............... 55.00
Petition to revive unintentionally abandoned application .... 1,320.00 ............. 660.00
Petitions related to provisional applications ........................... 50.00

*Remittances from foreign countries must be payable and immediately negotiable in the United States for the full amount of the fee required.*

# 3. References

*Manual of Patent Examining Procedure*, U.S. Government Printing Office.
*Rules of Practice in Patent Cases*, Title 37, Code of Federal Regulations, U.S. Government Printing Office.
*Desk Encyclopedia of Intellectual Property*, J. T. McCarthy, Bureau of National Affairs, 1991.
*The Mechanics of Patent Claim Drafting*, J. C. Landis, 3rd Edition, Practicing Law Institute, 1990.
*Patent Litigation Ptocedure and Tactics*, R. S. White, Matthew Bender, 1990.
*Patent Licensing Transactions—Forms*, C. Einhorn, Matthew Bender, 1990.
*Drafting Patent License Agreements*, 3rd Edition, Mayers & Brunsrold, BNA, 1991.
*Patents Throughout the World*, A. M. Greene, Clark Boardmen, 1980.
*Complete guide to Making Money with Your Ideas and Inventions*, R. E. Paige, Barnes & Noble, New York, 1976.
*Pratt's Guide to Venture Capital Sources*, Venture Economics, Inc., 1991.
*The Insider's Guide to Small Business Resources*, David E. Gumpert and Jeffrey A. Timmons, Doubleday, 1982.
*The Trademark Guide*, Lee Wilson, Allworth Press, 1996.
*The Copyright Guide*, Lee Wilson, Allworth Press, 1996.
*Guide to American Directories*, 9th Edition, B. Kleon Publishers, New York, 1975.

**Small Business Administration Publications and Publication Number**
*Thinking About Going into Business* (MA 2.025)
*Checklist for Going into Business* (MA 2.016)
*Ideas into Dollars* (SBB 91)
*Selecting the Legal Structure for Your Business* (MA 6.004)
*Marketing for Small Business* (SBB 89)
*Keeping Records in Small Business* (MA 1.017)
*Small Business Bibliography* (No. 15)

# Index

## Books from Allworth Press

**The Copyright Guide** by Lee Wilson (softcover, 6 × 9, 192 pages, $18.95)

**The Trademark Guide** by Lee Wilson (softcover, 6 × 9, 192 pages, $18.95)

**Legal-Wise: Self-Help Legal Guide for Everyone**,
Third Edition by Carl W. Battle (softcover, 8½ × 11, 208 pages, $18.95)

**Your Living Trust and Estate Plan: How to Maximize Your Family's Assets and Protect Your Loved Ones** by Harvey J. Platt
(softcover, 6 × 9, 256 pages, $14.95)

**Immigration Questions and Answers**, Revised Edition by Carl R. Baldwin
(softcover, 6 × 9, 176 pages, $14.95)

**Hers: The Wise Woman's Guide to Starting a Business on $2,000 or Less** by Carol Milano (softcover, 6 × 9, 224 pages, $16.95)

**Licensing Art and Design**, Revised Edition by Caryn R. Leland
(softcover, 128 pages, $16.95)

**The Internet Research Guide** by Timothy K. Maloy
(softcover, 6 × 9, 208 pages, $18.95)

**The Internet Publicity Guide** by V. A. Shiva
(softcover, 6 × 9, 208 pages, $18.95)

**The Writer's Legal Guide** by Tad Crawford and Tony Lyons
(softcover, 6 × 9, 304 pages, $19.95)

**Business and Legal Forms for Authors and Self-Publishers**,
Revised Edition by Tad Crawford (softcover, 8½ × 11, 192 pages, $19.95)

Please write to request our free catalog. If you wish to order a book, send your check or money order to Allworth Press, 10 East 23rd Street, Suite 210, New York, NY 10010. Include $5 for shipping and handling for the first book ordered and $1 for each additional book. Ten dollars plus $1 for each additional book if ordering from Canada. New York State residents must add sales tax.

If you wish to see our catalog on the World Wide Web, you can find us at Millennium Production's Art and Technology Web site: **http://www.arts-online.com/allworth/home.html** or at **allworth.com**